CASSANDRA

Pierre de Ronsard was born near Vendôme in France in 1524. After his diplomatic career was ended by illness he entered holy orders in 1543. In 1550 he published his *Odes*, followed in 1552 by *Les Amours de Cassandre*, which established him as the outstanding poet in French of his time, acknowledged leader of the group now known as the 'Pléiade'. One of the great poets of the European Renaissance, numbering writers, scholars, kings and queens (including Mary Queen of Scots and Elizabeth I) amongst his admirers, he published a vast oeuvre right up to his death in 1585.

Clive Lawrence was born in 1969 and graduated from Downing College, Cambridge in 1990. He has worked in the legal profession in Yorkshire since 1991. In 2011 he was joint winner of the John Dryden Prize awarded by the British Comparative Literature Association and the British Centre for Literary Translation (University of East Anglia) for translations of Pierre de Ronsard.

Fyfield*Books* aim to make available some of the great classics of British and European literature in clear, affordable formats, and to restore often neglected writers to their place in literary tradition.

Fyfield*Books* take their name from the Fyfield elm in Matthew Arnold's 'Scholar Gypsy' and 'Thyrsis'. The tree stood not far from the village where the series was originally devised in 1971.

> *Roam on! The light we sought is shining still.*
> *Dost thou ask proof? Our tree yet crowns the hill,*
> *Our Scholar travels yet the loved hill-side*

from 'Thyrsis'

PIERRE DE RONSARD

Cassandra

Translated and edited with an introduction by
CLIVE LAWRENCE

Fyfield*Books*
CARCANET

First published in Great Britain in 2015 by
Carcanet Press Limited
Alliance House
Cross Street
Manchester M2 7AQ

www.carcanet.co.uk

FSC
www.fsc.org
MIX
Paper from
responsible sources
FSC® C014540

A CIP catalogue record for this book is available from the British Library

ISBN 978 1 78410 010 0

The publisher acknowledges financial assistance from Arts Council England

Supported by
ARTS COUNCIL
ENGLAND

Typeset by XL Publishing Services, Exmouth
Printed and bound in England by SRP Ltd, Exeter

CONTENTS

INTRODUCTION

A Renaissance Project

When in 1552 Pierre de Ronsard published *Les Amours de Cassandre,* a sonnet sequence rooted in the Petrarchan tradition, his first readers might have expressed some surprise. He had begun his public career as a poet at the age of 26 only two years earlier, with the publication of four books of Odes openly designed to break with the recent past of French poetry. Quite apart from their intrinsic value as poems, these Odes were examples set by Ronsard to champion the domestication into French of classical models such as the Odes of Pindar and Horace, in preference to following poets of the previous century such as Villon and Charles d'Orléans in the use of medieval forms such as 'rondeaux, ballades, virelais', which Ronsard and associates such as Joachim Du Bellay saw as signs of corruption in the language and of ignorance in the literary culture.

The success of these Odes with an influential and elite readership established Ronsard at the head of a classicising avant-garde of young poets who shared a humanist education and a certain contempt for their poetic predecessors such as Clément Marot and Mellin de Saint-Gelais. This new wave of poets, who called themselves 'La Brigade', and whom (following Saint-Beuve) we now often refer to as 'La Pléiade', saw these fashionable authors as the writers of a facile, merely decorative court verse who failed to treat French poetry with the high seriousness and dignity it deserved and demanded.

In his polemical preface to the Odes, a provocative piece of literary coat-trailing, Ronsard proclaimed Pindar as his model, and aimed a passing shot at the courtiers 'who admire nothing save a little *Petrarchised* sonnet', perhaps as a form of retaliation in advance for the neglect such learned and 'difficult' poetry could expect in court circles. He was careful however to include

formal compliments to influential contemporaries and imme-
diate predecessors such as Marot, Scève and Saint-Gelais,
exempting them from the general censure and showing
(however much his tongue may have been in his cheek amid
some otherwise inflammatory language) some mastery of
literary politics. The objective of the Odes and the poetry they
advocated and exemplified was nonetheless clear: to take
French poetry out of what La Brigade considered its decorative
time-warp of trivial compliment and courtly flattery and to
instil into it the epic scope and ambition of the Ancients.

As a result, when *Les Amours de Cassandre* was published
alongside the fifth and final book of Ronsard's Odes, the
apparent transfer of allegiance it implied, from Pindar to
Petrarch, the classical to the medieval, the humanist intellec-
tuals to the butterflies of the court, might have raised a few
eyebrows.

Yet *Les Amours de Cassandre* was far more than just a new
flavour introduced into Ronsard's evolving poetic career. It was
a project that would help to define him as a poet, and go far
beyond the coterie success of the Odes in establishing his status
as one of the greatest poets of the European Renaissance. It is
in many ways an archetypal Renaissance project, a synthesis of
the best of the available traditions that combined the spiritu-
ality and inwardness of the Petrarchan tradition with the
sensuality and mythological grandeur of the classical and
Neo-Latin poets. Ronsard and his 'Lady', Cassandre, as the
protagonists of the work, are depicted as intensely alive, and
(for all their participation in the familiar configurations of the
Petrarchan tradition) as individual people, lovers acting as
physical, emotional and intellectual beings in a natural world
governed by the material processes of change, movement and
time that they themselves share and exhibit.

To the template of the Petrarchan sonnet sequence, recurring
themes from classical mythology (and in particular Ovid's
theme of metamorphosis) add a flesh-and-blood sensuality and
a sense of the numinous intervention, through nature, of the
divine in this world; and Neo-Platonism overlays a philosoph-
ical, spiritualised intellectual scheme that imports elements of

Christian mysticism and exalted ideas of poetic inspiration. The result is an enriching fusion whereby the lovers transcend the intimacy of their relations to become epic figures, sharing a mythical register and by metamorphosis partaking of the processes of the material world, while at the same time struggling with, fulfilling or failing their spiritual destinies both as individuals and as a couple.

The status of this work in Ronsard's vast oeuvre can be seen by the arrangement of the many editions of his Collected Poems he supervised from 1560 to 1584, the year before his death. Rather than adopt a chronological plan, Ronsard came to group his poems by form: sonnet sequences, hymns, odes, occasional poems and so forth. Reworkings and re-orderings constantly took place as the oeuvre evolved as a whole, but, while not immune to such alterations itself, *Les Amours de Cassandre*, whether entitled simply as the First Book of *Les Amours* or by reference to Cassandre, always retained its integrity as a distinct work at the head of the sequences of love sonnets, and took pride of place at the beginning of Ronsard's final edition of his works in 1584.

Ronsard would go on to be the great serial monogamist of the sonnet sequence – future sonnets and sonnet sequences would be written to Marie, Astrée, Hélène, and others. This later apparent contradiction of his professions of undying love to Cassandre was accompanied by his statements of frank disbelief that the great exemplar of the love sonneteers, Petrarch, never slept with his beloved, Laura – if he was not getting sex then he should have moved on, as Ronsard himself did after Cassandre. The later sonnet sequences develop Ronsard's art yet further, and approach both the relationship with the beloved they depict and the nature of love poetry itself in different ways. In its own terms, the *Amours de Cassandre* remains unique in Ronsard's work: it is not simply the first attempt in a genre further perfected in his later career. Ronsard, as inveterate a tinkerer with his published poetry as later poets such as Yeats and Auden, would continue to alter and reform it throughout his career as an autonomous and self-contained collection, and to retain the qualities that differentiate it from its successor sequences. The present translation is of the final and conclusive version of the sequence assembled from 1578 and published in the final collected works of 1584, representing Ronsard's last thoughts after half a lifetime of additions and revisions.

In some ways, Ronsard's early life and training, and the radical change of direction circumstances forced upon him in his youth, were the perfect preparation for a poet who would fuse such disparate elements as those that make up *Les Amours de Cassandre*. To understand the sources of the work, the contexts that gave rise to it and the poet who wrote it, some background from Ronsard's early life, and an outline of the story behind Ronsard's contacts with the woman conjectured to be the real, historical Cassandre, may be useful.

Ronsard's Early Life

Ronsard was born on 2nd September 1524 at his family's estate, La Possonnière, in the Loire valley between Château de Loire and Vendôme. His family were landowners and courtiers who owed their increased prominence and wealth in the two generations preceding Pierre's birth to close links to the French Crown. Ronsard's father, Loys (commonly modernised to Louis), was a man of broad culture and himself a keen amateur poet. In the decade prior to Pierre's birth Louis had rebuilt La Possonnière on the model of the Renaissance buildings he had seen while on military service in Italy. Pierre was the youngest of four children and the third son.

Shortly after Pierre was born the French King François I was captured by the Holy Roman Emperor Charles V at the Battle of Pavia. To secure his own release, he was forced to enter into the Treaty of Madrid, one of the results of which was the offer of his two eldest sons, François and Henri, as hostages in his place. It is a mark of the respect in which Louis de Ronsard was held by the French Crown that he was selected to accompany the two young princes into their captivity to Spain, where he and they would ultimately spend more than four years from 1526. The main paternal influence in Pierre's earliest years while Louis was away seems to have been his uncle, Jean, a churchman and humanist who on his death, tellingly, left his nephew his library. Louis, on his return, sought to give to his youngest son the modern education he had seen given to the princes in Spain. At the age of nine, Pierre, in whom his father had detected signs of great intellectual ability, was sent to the College of Navarre. There the intention would doubtless have been that he would not only receive an academic education, but also grow up in the company of many sons of the great families of France who would form an extended network of contacts at the highest levels throughout the rest of his life. However, this scheme does not seem immediately to have borne fruit. Ronsard soon left the College.

Notwithstanding that false start, Louis's plans are not difficult to decipher. Given his position as a youngest son, Pierre's future would be one through which he would have to make his own path. He was therefore to be educated to the life of the courtier in the manner fitting the Renaissance court of the brilliant François I: to combine learning and the cultivation of the arts with the military tradition inherited from the feudal past. Pierre appears to have been admirably suited to the life. By 1536 he was beginning the career of a courtier, for which the training was provided by the Ecurie du Roi, which should be considered as Ronsard's next educational establishment, the place where he could be immersed in the milieu in which it was intended he would spend his adult life. He began as a page first to the Dauphin, François, then to his brother Charles, and then to their sister, Madeleine. This final transfer of his services coincided with the arrangements for a marriage between Madeleine and James V of Scotland, and would bring Ronsard in the following year in her entourage to Scotland.

The marriage was important diplomatically, but Madeleine's health was too weak from tuberculosis for there to be any great optimism concerning her long-term survival in the harsher climate of Scotland. 'The Summer Queen of Forty Days', she died in Edinburgh on 7th July 1537. Thereafter, while James V pursued negotiations for another marriage with the royal house of France (which would culminate in his marrying Mary of

Guise, the future Regent and mother of Mary Queen of Scots), Ronsard and his fellow French courtiers kicked their heels in Scotland. For a British reader, it is an intriguing time in the poet's life, about which not enough is known. He and the French contingent seem to have spent the next year, until their departure under safe passage through England in July 1538, at St Andrews: what he did during a year of enforced idleness is open to conjecture, but he had already shown an aptitude and taste for literature, and the presence of the university there makes it unlikely that this was a time wholly wasted.

On his return to France Ronsard rejoined the entourage of Charles, Duc d'Orléans, the favourite son of François I. The next couple of years saw him involved in a minor, but growing, diplomatic role in the factional struggles of the French court and the wider European rivalries between François I, the Holy Roman Emperor Charles V and Henry VIII of England. He was clearly considered a promising diplomat, and seemed set fair to pursue the all-round ideals of the Renaissance, as intellectual, soldier, amateur versifier and athlete: he easily held his own in the competitive machismo of the military and equestrian exploits of the court, and even much later in his life his skill as a footballer helped on occasions to keep him in high favour with the French Crown.

Illness and Change of Direction

In 1541, however, everything changed. While still in his teens Ronsard suffered a serious illness. What exactly it was we do not know. The biographer's favourite stand-by for any illness that does not yield to immediate modern diagnosis, syphilis, has been mentioned as a candidate, picking up on some contemporary libels. Some form of rheumatic fever has also been suggested. Whatever this illness was, however, it is clear that this was a major, life-changing setback that affected Ronsard's health and constitution for the rest of his days. It impaired his hearing and was said to have made him unsuitable for diplomatic life. The extent to which that holds water is perhaps debatable: he was left 'hard of hearing' rather than entirely deaf, and while it was said at the time that this made him unable to do a job that consisted largely in the picking up of backstairs whispers, there may have been other, political factors connected with factional in-fighting at the French court that helped to account for the radical change of direction Ronsard next took.

After a lengthy convalescence, Ronsard appears to have agreed a new life strategy with his father. The relationship between Louis and Pierre seems to have been a good one, between a father fond of his gifted youngest child and a precocious son slightly in awe of a figure who had remained somewhat distant, for all his affection. There was no need on either side for the revolt and oppression of the Romantic poet's biography. Both seemed to have a healthy dose of pragmatism: and consequently, on 6th March 1543 Ronsard received the tonsure from the Bishop of Le Mans in his father's presence.

This new status as a tonsured cleric, the lowest rung of Holy Orders, needs to be seen in context. It was not a calling to the Church in the way we might understand that now. To be tonsured was to be admitted into an estate in life where Church benefices became available to you. The vows you took could be renounced, particularly useful in the case of a younger son who might be called upon for one reason or another to supply a family with heirs.

Ronsard had taken an alternative path to the patronage he would seek as a poet, by opening up the possibility of receiving the livings the Church afforded to those who, nominally or in substance, became the effective directors of Church institutions by taking on the roles of abbots, priors and the like. Now, looking to exploit the intellectual and literary gifts he had not so far developed to the full, he was sent to Paris to receive the most rigorous of humanist educations with Lazare de Baïf and Jean Dorat in a kind of informal university based at Les Tournelles. He had accompanied Baïf on a diplomatic mission in 1540 and might have identified himself as promising in the eyes of the great scholar then. Now it was time for Ronsard to receive the comprehensive grounding in Latin, Greek, literature and philosophy he had so far lacked in his acquisition of the fashionable smatterings regarded as preparation for the life of a courtier. He started a long way behind his often much younger classmates, and was often helped out by the far more advanced Jean-Antoine de Baïf, natural son of Lazare and some eight or nine years his junior. That Ronsard caught up so much so quickly is a tribute as much to the intensive nature of the education he received as to his ability to assimilate it.

However, the time with Baïf and Dorat gave him much more than a good knowledge of Latin and Greek. Through them and their connections Ronsard became part of a network of similarly educated young men – Jean-Antoine de Baïf, Joachim Du Bellay, Remy Belleau, Pontus de Tyard, Marc-Antoine de Muret – who would form the nucleus of La Brigade or the Pléiade, the new 'movement' in French poetry he would lead throughout his career. Other contacts made at the same time, including the future Protestant reformer Theodore du Bèze, would crop up on numerous occasions in his later life. It was a network of intellectuals to rival and complement the network of rising court officials and aristocrats he had inherited from his family and then developed in his education for, and short experience of, life as a courtier.

Ronsard's way was now further committed by the death in 1545 of his protector and patron in court circles, Charles, the Duc d'Orléans. While that by no means made him an unwelcome stranger to the court, it helped to determine the capacity in which he would appear there: it was now more or less settled for him that literature and the Church would be his future and represent his principal claims to preferment. The disabilities left to him by his illness could be accommodated and worked around, and the disadvantages of the youngest son without expectations of property, or any realistic prospect of royal employment, could be offset by literary talent and the skills his disparate experiences in youth had given him.

Brought up amongst the children of the great aristocrats in a military and courtly milieu; accustomed to and at home with the manners, interests and politics of a Renaissance court, having excelled in its strenuous pastimes and been blooded in its manoeuvrings; educated then amongst the leading humanists of his day; a man of flesh and blood, one who had suffered the disadvantages of the younger son, debilitating illness and disappointed ambitions, while at the same time having been in some sense liberated by those circumstances into being able to pursue literature: Ronsard was ready to begin his literary career.

Cassandra Salviati

The Lady of these sonnets, Cassandre, has long been identified as a real, historical woman, Cassandra Salviati. The extent to which she is really the Cassandre of the *Amours de Cassandre* remains controversial. Against such an identification is the paucity of contemporary comment about it, and some suggestive counter-evidence in the poetry. Prior to the *Amours de Cassandre* Ronsard had written poems to a Cassandre who did not seem to share the characteristics of the Cassandre of the sonnets, being apparently an altogether easier-going object of affection than the Petrarchan ideal depicted in the *Amours*. The Cassandre of the *Amours* also seems at times to share the physical characteristics and the actions of more than one woman – for instance, the general depiction of her is of a blonde woman with brown eyes, but there are other references that raise questions even over such general details. Certain sonnets seem to be written about or to another woman and in or about a different relationship altogether. It may be, therefore, that even where real-life circumstances are used directly in the poems, those are attributed to 'Cassandre' as a generic name for the loved woman. Indeed, it was said by some of his contemporaries, including his first biographer Binet (who knew him personally towards the end of his life) that he fell in love more with the name 'Cassandre', full of tragic and epic connotations, than with the woman. The resonance of that name and all it brought with it certainly forms a major element of the poems, and its adoption may result more from conscious choice than convenient accident.

Together, these factors lead to the suggestion by some critics that 'Cassandre' is a fiction lent a potent name from a woman met in passing, and that what Ronsard needed for *Les Amours de Cassandre* was not a real-life love affair to record so much as a locus upon which the various literary conventions he would use and subvert could concentre. 'Cassandre' is Cassandra Salviati in the same way that 'Stella' is Penelope Rich in Sir Philip Sidney's *Astrophil and Stella*, for instance.

Set against that there is a persistent interest in the real-world transactions that are or may be traceable between Ronsard and Cassandra Salviati. She was the daughter of an Italian banker who had made his home in France, the master of the Château de Talcy which sits not far from Ronsard's home in the surroundings of the Loire Valley. (Ronsard's 'home' river, as he makes clear, was the Loir, a different river from the Loire – see sonnet CCVII). Ronsard met her when he was twenty and she was fifteen, in 1545 at a ball at Blois (see sonnet XVIII). On this version of events, aided by Ronsard's references in the sonnets to the duration of his love and the particulars he gives of their first meeting (such as in sonnet CXV), his love or attraction for her can be dated back to this first sight. At least, even if only for the name, Cassandra Salviati seems to have stuck in his mind. Ronsard would hardly be the last to parlay a momentary attraction to a woman into a relationship played out only in the theatre of the imagination: but we have to remain open to the possibility that there could have been more to it than that.

At this point in his life Ronsard was young and comparatively obscure, certainly not yet the famous poet. His family was good, but he was a third son, a tonsured cleric, something even of a perpetual student, and had suffered from ill health. Even if there was a genuine attachment between them, the idea that there could be any suggestion of official courtship or marriage between M. de Ronsard and Mlle de Talcy would have been ridiculous. In November 1546 Cassandra married one Jean III de Peigné, a local aristocrat with land to offer. Their direct descendants would include another French poet of note, Alfred de Musset.

Cassandra and her husband lived at his estate at Pray not far from Ronsard's family home of La Possonnière and shared some of the same social circles with the Ronsard family: there is evidence that there was some form of ongoing contact between her and Ronsard, probably including a visit by her and her husband to La Possonnière at the time the sonnets were being written. The highly anecdotal nature of some of the sonnets may be evidence that they contain stylisations of actual events. The very specific location of certain of the sonnets in place and time and contemporary references to events of 1552 may add some further justification to such a reading. There are also suggestions that there could have been further contact between Ronsard and Cassandra in later life around 1569, and possibly even later thereafter.

Where the truth ultimately lies can only be conjectured, and the side on which critics come down seems to be dictated in many instances less by the evidence within the poems or extraneous to them than by that critic's attitude to biographical criticism and the sources of poetic inspiration. The modern fashion is to disclaim the direct autobiographical meaning of works such as *Les Amours de Cassandre*, just as the Victorians and their successors loved to extrapolate them into romanticised novellas in which asexual ciphers would romp through the fantasies of celibate scholars. If called upon to throw in my own view, for what it may be worth, I would suggest that the facts probably lie somewhere in the middle: there may have been a number of meetings, events, exchanges between Ronsard and Cassandra Salviati, and some of what appears in these poems, be it physical description or narrative, may have some ultimate basis in reality. There may have been an element of sexual attraction between Ronsard and Cassandra: some of it may even have been mutual. There may have been a romantic or flirtatious friendship. That there was no true sexual relationship is made clear by Ronsard. But the Cassandre of the poems is a fully fictional figure in a work of conscious artifice and artistry, an idealised projection, albeit possibly from some hints in reality, just as the landscape behind her is mythologised beyond the mere topography of the Vendôme region. Like Petrarch's Laura, she is more a manifestation of the 'Eternal Feminine' as conceived by Ronsard than the girlfriend he couldn't keep.

That is where the question of the real-life relationship between the two has to rest, in the absence of further evidence, and in the full realisation that any writer of Ronsard's sophistication was more than capable of playing whatever games with truth and interpretation he chose in laying paths and pitfalls in his work. The relationship between the two in the poems, however, is what matters four hundred and sixty-odd years on, and is very much open to exploration.

In any event, the extent to which *Les Amours de Cassandre* has genuine roots in autobiography, though interesting, is in the final analysis relatively unimportant. What can be said, however, is that, whatever variant of initial attraction and continuing emotional attachment on Ronsard's part existed, when allied to the clear practical impossibility of the relationship going any further, it led to a perfect poetic opportunity. In *Les Amours de Cassandre* Ronsard selects and uses the elements before him to unify his poetic interests in the evolution of a transcendent fiction. That he is entirely aware of doing so is constantly evident: the Renaissance poets have plenty left to teach the postmodernists in terms of ludic self-awareness.

It is a trite observation to make that in the act of writing writers express themselves to some extent, while to another they discover and create themselves in the act of expression: every writer's characteristic approach falls, and every literary work derives its origin, somewhere on the graph between those two apparent extremes. Ronsard appears to be one of those writers whose emotional intensity and the intensity he is capable of expressing are one and the same thing: his ability to create and his ability to feel are directly related, and it is purely simplistic psychology to suggest that the traffic from emotion to expression only travels in one direction. It goes both ways: in fact, it creates a circle. Put in its bluntest form: if Ronsard was not in love with this girl helpfully named after a Greek mythological heroine before he started work, he could write himself into whatever state he needed to occupy for the poetry he wanted to write.

Later Life

Ronsard's status as the leading French poet of his time was acquired early and never seriously challenged in the French court circles where he established his base. 'Prince of Poets, Poet of Princes' was an epithet applied to him in his own lifetime, and reflects how close he remained to the French Crown through the entirety of his career, through all the evolutions and changes of a turbulent time. He wrote 'official' verses, although with a reservation of individualism, an irony, and an occasional eloquent silence, that speak to his independence of spirit, and he acquired and swapped benefices to build substantial possessions in and around his beloved Vendôme. One of these, the Priory of Saint-Cosme near Tours, where he died and was buried in 1585, still exists and can be visited. While it was a life of relentless activity, controversy and literary production, one constantly immersed in a fractured and tormented time, there are few of the usual biographical landmarks to record.

The history of France throughout Ronsard's adult life was dominated by the Wars of Religion, as Protestants and Catholics fought through France war after war, with such atrocities as the St Bartholomew's Day Massacre as testimony to the murderous intensity of the hatreds that were unleashed. Ronsard, as a Catholic cleric and royal poet, could not remain isolated from the controversies and accompanying pamphlet wars of the time. His initial attempt at statesmanlike moderation somewhat crumbled in the face of the vicious personal attacks he suffered at the hands of Protestant propagandists, and, in perhaps their most provocative move, their persistent suggestion that, in Guillaume de Salluste Du Bartas, the Protestant faction had a poet greater than Ronsard. The interventions made by Ronsard into the pamphlet and propaganda wars of the time, such as *Discours des Misères de Ce Temps*, provide yet another dimension to a poetic career that explored a multitude of forms and registers, from a semi-abortive epic, *La Franciade*, via odes, hymns, elegies and eclogues to public poetry in the form of occasional poems, discourses and epitaphs.

The final collected works, collected and collated with

immense care by Ronsard throughout his career, mark him as one of the great Renaissance writers and one of the leading poets in French literature, vastly admired in his own time, and, although eclipsed and largely disregarded during the lengthy 'classical' phase of French literature, rediscovered and re-launched by critics of the nineteenth century such as Saint-Beuve. He was admired by even so fastidious a reader as Flaubert, who declared him in his correspondence to be greater than Virgil and the equal of Goethe. In modern times his reputation is secure, with numerous editions of his poetry available and a vast scholarly literature. He has been referred to as one of the 'big three' of French sixteenth-century literature, alongside Rabelais, whom he appears to have known and on whom he wrote a vigorous epitaph, and Montaigne, who refers to him with admiration.

The Strategies of *Les Amours de Cassandre*

As seen above, Ronsard's preface to the Odes of 1550 had scorned the prevailing Petrarchan style adopted by the courtier poets of his time and joined Du Bellay's influential 'manifesto' for the Pléiade poets, *Défense et Illustration de la Langue Française*, in its rejection of the medieval forms. In fact, it is probable that Ronsard collaborated on the *Défence* with Du Bellay. The analogy with Wordsworth and Coleridge working on the Preface to *Lyrical Ballads* is highly inexact but irresistible. In this document, the author or authors are clearly picking a fight: it is deliberately provocative. Its main objectives are to advocate the fitness of French as a literary language against those who felt that, as a mere vernacular, it could never rival Latin or Greek in its range of expression, and to exhort those who wrote in French to help build it into a language capable of acting as a medium for great literature. This would be achieved by following the example of great classical authors, while rejecting the trivial and corrupt poetry of the court with its reliance on nostalgic forms and subjects. The rudeness here and in Ronsard's preface towards the court as a literary centre is striking: maybe Ronsard in particular was keen to vindicate his new path against that from which circumstances had excluded him. But that is simply speculation.

The Odes themselves marked a new departure in French poetry, with Ronsard marking himself out as the leader of an avant-garde, classicising group, in the tradition of, and claiming authority from, epic poets such as Homer, Virgil and Ovid, and lyric poets such as Pindar and Horace. Rejecting the option taken by many humanist poets of writing in Latin, Ronsard had taken on instead the project advocated in the *Défence* of domesticating into French vernacular poetry the best his classical models had to teach, to give French poetry a corresponding reach and dignity.

So why then in 1552 did the leading poet of this new classical school apparently perform a volte-face and write a sonnet sequence that not only clearly shows an extensive knowledge of Petrarch but manifestly is designed as a work in that tradition? Had Ronsard gone over to the enemy? Had he deserted the humanist intellectuals and joined the court faction to advance his temporal interests? Was Ronsard playing to the court here, to win back friends and potential benefactors he may have alienated with his difficult and mythologically dense Odes, or, perhaps more dangerously, with the corrosive sarcasm of his preface? Was this just politics and patronage?

The first point to make here is that the apparent opposition between the factions is easy to oversimplify and overstate. For all Ronsard's contempt for the French Petrarchan poets of his day, that contempt did not extend to Petrarch's work itself. The *Défence* had clearly held out Petrarch's work as being another fruitful model for the new French poetry, and as a poet Du Bellay himself anticipated Ronsard with his own sonnet sequence, *L'Olive*, published alongside the *Défence* in 1549. There was not a simple binary opposition between the classicisers and the Petrarchans, but a subtler and more nuanced difference of opinion and approach relating to many issues, amongst them the manner in which Petrarch's influence should be assimilated into French.

Nonetheless, by assimilating and appropriating Petrarch in

his own way, Ronsard pulled off a bold flanking manoeuvre in the literary politics of the day. It could also be seen as a skilful move in the court politics of the time to which Ronsard would owe most of his future hopes of patronage: it enabled him to nuance his previously hostile stance towards the court and its Petrarchan literary fashions, to join in rather than remain out in the cold, while at the same time consolidating his position at the head of the avant-garde. It allowed him also to mend fences with influential court poets such as Mellin de Saint-Gelais, whose influence could otherwise have stood in the way of his career.

The result was a considerable success for Ronsard, cementing his position as the leading poet of his day and eclipsing the elders his lip-service had helped to disarm. In 1553, a new edition of *Les Amours de Cassandre*, including new additions to and re-orderings of the sonnets, was issued, accompanied now by a commentary by Ronsard's friend Marc-Antoine de Muret. While the purpose of this commentary was doubtless principally to guide readers through the mythological thickets of learned allusions, it was also an opportunity to flaunt the erudition of the poetry, to give the allure of difficulty at the same time as seeking to dispel its reality. One is reminded of the annotations to their works by modern poets such as Eliot, Empson and Bunting, which often have the effect less of explication than of increasing the poetry's suggestive range. Like the poems it accompanied, the commentary continued to evolve over time, even at times when Muret could not feasibly have been involved, and it has been conjectured that Ronsard himself began to use this ventriloquial method to shape the perception of the poems as new editions were issued.

The Poetry of *Les Amours de Cassandre*

In purely formal terms, *Les Amours de Cassandre* is a sonnet sequence, with a few interpolated songs and lyrics and, at the conclusion, several extended 'Elegies' in a markedly more relaxed and sometimes ironic register. The 229 sonnets are dense with allusions to, quotations from and translations of not only Petrarch, whose manner, style and subject matter dominate the sequence, but also other Italian lyric poets such as Ariosto and Bembo, Latin poets such as Catullus, Horace and Ovid, Neo-Latin poets such as Marullus, and many more.

This is not, however, just a library poetry, a Petrarchan commonplace book stuffed with learned borrowings. From the very outset, it demonstrates a high level of lyric and dramatic intensity. Quite aside from the literary and critical, even political, interests it serves, it stands on its own account as poetry with a powerful and vivid voice, a fresh articulacy and complexity, offering a simultaneous examination of the nature of strong emotion and the capacity of literature and poetry to embody it. These are highly literary and allusive poems, written for a sophisticated and knowing audience, by an ambitious writer keen to secure his literary, political and material success, which communicate genuine feeling and lived experience with a power seldom seen before or since.

As a conscious innovator, Ronsard is not only showing the breadth of his knowledge and reference, he is also choosing his literary ancestors in a similar way to the early Modernists in English such as Eliot and Pound, who used a number of the same tactics. By choosing forebears in this way, you get to appropriate the parts of the tradition you want to your project. Every self-styled revolution chooses its own pantheon and derives its own apostolic succession. (This kinship may even be one of the factors behind Pound's explicit reference to Ronsard's 'Ode pour l'Élection de son Sépulcre' in *Hugh Selwyn Mauberley*, written when he and Eliot went back to regular rhyme and metre after what they saw as the excesses of the first period of *vers libre*.)

In this way, therefore, Ronsard gets to add nuance to his disapproval of Petrarchan imitators as expressed in the past, claims Petrarch as his own ancestor in this richer mix of influences, assimilates Petrarch to the new poetry and appropriates that potent legacy, while managing to straddle the divide he himself had been instrumental in creating. And all the while he blends the disparate elements from which this poetry is formed

xxiii

into an instrument capable of levels of complexity and intensity that justify the claims he makes for it.

All this may seem a little dry in considering what is, after all, intense love poetry. However, to be appreciated fully, *Les Amours de Cassandre* should be seen as the poetry of an extensively engaged poet who played a prominent part in an intensely politicised and social milieu, one in which humanist learning threatened medieval intellectual habits and fashions just as Protestantism threatened the verities of a Catholic nation. The politics of literature were a subsidiary part of the same series of struggles. At the same time as he writes passionately of love and its consequences, Ronsard is consciously pioneering a new literature as part of the intellectual project of his time.

The Elements Fused

Extensive and intense though the imitation of and influence by Petrarch may be, that element perhaps should be seen as the basic background literary template for *Les Amours de Cassandre* rather than the model that the work was designed ultimately to emulate. It has been suggested that, for the Renaissance poet, imitation of Petrarch was the persona one adopted to be a poet of love. Ronsard's use of the standard ingredients of Petrarchanism, the way that they connect fruitfully with his other themes and influences, shows that they are not simply collected and trotted out but are creatively integrated into his imaginative universe.

On top of that Petrarchan background Ronsard places a further layer of classical influence. The name 'Cassandra', which Ronsard was accused of loving more than the girl, provided a reference to one of the great tragic heroines of the Trojan War. Cassandra, daughter of Priam, King of Troy, rejected the advances of Apollo, god of prophecy. In revenge, Apollo granted her wish to have prophetic powers, but added the proviso that, although her prophecies would be true, no one would believe them. Cassandra's prophecies were duly ignored by the rulers of Troy, and she is later seen as one of the victims of the Greek sack of the city.

Ronsard makes frequent reference to this story, to the links therefore between himself and Apollo (also, it will be recalled, the god of poetry) in their capacity as lovers of 'Cassandra', to the numerous connected stories and myths, and to the themes suggested by the attributes of Apollo whose influence as a god extended over poetic inspiration and prophecy, the sun, sickness and healing. The repeated use of these narratives and frames of reference imports into the sequence a further layer of influence and meaning: the epic and mythological. See, for instance, sonnets IV, XXIV, XXXIII, XXXVI, CV and CXXIII.

This is one of the ways in which *Les Amours de Cassandre* connects with the Odes. Ronsard has not abandoned the objective of bringing to French poetry an epic grandeur by the imitation and adoption of the classical authors, and here he extends that project to the field of love poetry. Myths are constantly invoked, whether they be the tales of the Trojan War, linking to Homer, or the full range of mythical stories that link to Catullus, Propertius, Tibullus and the entire gamut of classical literature. See, for instance, sonnets IV, XXXII, XXXVI, XLIV, LXXVII, LXXXVII, CV, CXXXIII, CXLVII, CXC and CCXXIII. The most important poet and exemplar in this context is Ovid.

Central to the entire work are themes of metamorphosis, taken at least in part from Ovid's *Metamorphoses*, which relates a series of numinous interchanges between the human and natural world and the divine by way of transformation. See, for instance, sonnets IX, XVI, XX, XL, XC, CXVI, CLV, CLVII, CLXXXVI, CLXXXIX and CCXII. One of the main themes of *Les Amours de Cassandre* is that of the emotional metamorphoses caused by love and events that occur in the relationship of the lovers, and the physical changes that arise from the resulting psychological states. It is in that context that descriptions of change and movement from the natural world form a point of connection between other central elements of the work: the conventional metaphors and heightened emotional attitudes of Petrarchanism, the intensely experienced surroundings of the

Vendôme region in which the poems are set, the obsessive self-observation of the poet, the epic and mythological register of Ovid and the classical poets, and the sense of the interpenetration of the spiritual with the material world in a context of continuous 'becoming' highlighted by the numerous references to Neo-Platonism, which forms an important philosophical background to many of the poems: see, for instance, sonnets XXI, XXXI, LII, LXXXI, CI, CLXII, CLXXIX and CCV.

Neo-Platonism, as exemplified in the work of the Italian philosopher Marsilio Ficino (1433–99), is, to say the least, difficult to summarise, succinctly or at all. The following is necessarily a rough and approximate sketch of a few features of this philosophy that are relevant to *Les Amours de Cassandre*. Drawing on the work of Plato, it posits a world of spiritual essences beyond the phenomenal world we experience, one to which the individual is drawn in a path of self-perfection and to which he has access by way of transcendence of the mundane, through means that include the 'divine fury' of the inspired poet and the experience of love. In the spiritual experience of love, the lover confronts in the beloved an ideal presence largely of his own creation (perhaps with some resemblance to the Jungian idea of the 'anima'), through which he passes intellectually beyond the material world of illusions into an ineffable world of symbols and ideas in which lies an ultimate reality. This concept of the beloved as an experience of beauty transmuted in the soul of the lover to an ideal of perfection can be seen to run in some ways in harmony with the 'courtly love' conventions of Petrarchanism and to connect, amid constructive interference, both with the pagan, classical world of metamorphosis and with the actual physical world in which the sonnets are set, with its constant flux and movement, its constant changes of state.

Ronsard was a proud native of the Vendôme region and clearly the landscape and the sense of place available to him there were immensely important to him. An intense feeling for nature, hardly a commonplace in his time, is one of the most striking elements of the poetry he wrote throughout his life. See, for instance, sonnets IX, L, LIX, LX, LXVI, CXXIV, CXXXIV,

CLXV and CLXXIV. Ronsard's frequent withdrawals through-
out his career from Paris and the court back to the Vendôme
region are not just intermissions of rest, although doubtless they
served that purpose as well. They appeared also to be a way for
him to reconnect with the authenticity provided by his home-
land and what it brought with it: the life of the land, his family,
his personal history, the natural world.

In *Les Amours de Cassandre*, as in almost all of Ronsard's work,
the natural world is constantly evoked. Ronsard's Vendôme, its
landscapes, its weather, its seasons, its constant changes, are
like a character in the piece, or the orchestra in the song cycle.
It is both a real place, and a place generalised and idealised, like
a Poussin or Claude landscape, into a symbolic backdrop for
the events in the foreground. Its essential attribute of natural
movement, of natural change through time, is another instance
of a central theme throughout Ronsard's work. Everywhere
you look in *Les Amours de Cassandre* winds, seas and rivers
interact on each other, solids liquefy, liquids vaporise or
solidify, all manner of things form, dissolve, disintegrate or
seize up in stasis, dreams fade to reality, time runs or stands
still, substances and forces act and interact, change and inter-
change, war against and assimilate one another. This is how, for
Ronsard, the world works. But this perception also connects
again back to the theme of metamorphosis and becomes a
central theme of the sequence: the story of Cassandra and
Ronsard, rather than merely being the rarefied spiritual alle-
gory to which one interpretation of Petrarchanism, or
Neo-Platonism, might condemn it, is also one of two mortal
beings, flesh-and-blood lovers in the natural world of change,
mortality and decay.

Yet still this is a natural world out of Ovid and the mytho-
logical poets, one divinely touched by that magic that makes
the world and the experience of love numinous. The heighten-
ings and exaggerations in the depiction of the physical effects
of emotion, where weeping eyes let loose tears that turn to
rivers, hearts are consumed by fire and invaded by ice, sighs
give rise to storms, go beyond being mere copies of Petrarchan
conventions, with all their familiar stylisations: they also locate

Ronsard and Cassandra in the world of the *Metamorphoses* and so transpose them into the epic register, where human beings and gods inhabit and interact with a world that has the glamour and immanent meaning, the symbolic relevance to ourselves, the sense of the miraculous, that is our experience of it in the disorienting throes of intense love. The Neo-Platonic daimons and spirits that occur further identify that world as penetrable by the divine within a context that can be harmonised with Christian thought and ideas of poetic inspiration that were central to Ronsard's concept of poetry. These elements become central means for Ronsard of communicating the experience that love brings to human beings.

The combination of these elements and the kaleidoscopic way in which they circle around and merge with one another in changing alignments forms a principal way in which Ronsard works throughout the sequence. One paradigm overlays another to create a stereoscopic image. Different frames of reference and different conventions are followed, disrupted, superimposed, placed in apposition to one another: the result is to create a multiplicity of tones and dimensions that reproduces the psychological complexities and contradictions of the experience of love it describes.

This very tonal variety might make it seem as if there is something disjointed about the sequence, but this is not an accidental flaw. Ronsard uses these multiple tones and frames of reference to reproduce the discontinuities in mental state caused by the psychological disturbances of strong emotion, and the complex three-dimensional effect of one paradigm overlaying another to capture the ambivalence, the simultaneous experience of disparate or directly contradictory thoughts and emotions, that is part of the syndrome he is representing.

Attempts have been made to deduce a precise reason for the ordering of the sonnets, which Ronsard clearly cared about enough to alter it on occasion, in particular between the first edition of 1552 and the annotated edition in 1553. While some thematically linked shorter sequences within the overall sequence can be discerned, any all-encompassing pattern seems to elude analysis. There are, for instance, sonnets that date from,

or are presented as dating from, different times in the relation-
ship, by their various references to the time for which Ronsard
has been in love, scattered without discernible order through
the collection. Subsequent editions after 1553 incorporated
sonnets written considerably later. The real ordering principle
seems to include the intentional absence of a narrative order,
looking instead towards a more psychological and associative
pattern.

In these ways Ronsard reproduces and captures in the
texture of the work itself the paradoxical nature of extreme
emotion: its internal contradictions, its irreconcilable ideas and
feelings, its sudden changes of mood, its obsessive repetitions,
its constant adjustments and uncertainties. At the same time,
the high level of self-consciousness and control in the writing
depicts how strong feeling can coexist with irony and self-
awareness, how idealisation of the beloved can coexist with
deep disillusionment, obsessive compulsion with an acknowl-
edgement of being stuck, irrational fears with a sense of destiny,
self-loathing with resentment at one's ill-treatment, self-abase-
ment with ambition, hatred with desire. The result is a
compelling portrait of the mind under the pressure of strong
emotion.

At the same time we get a self-portrait of the author as one
who is aware of the ludic nature of literature, that all language
is fiction, and that both identity and memory are narrative and
therefore fictional and provisional. The consciously literary
nature of the work, drenched as it is in allusions, intertextuali-
ties, stock situations and well-known techniques, gives it a high
level of knowingness, a sense of the acceptance that there is
nothing new under the sun, only to each his own different
ordering and mixing of the constituent elements, and his own
inspiration in their deployment. Ronsard's use of his sources,
whether they are poetic conventions such as Petrarchanism,
philosophical ideas such as Neo-Platonism or persistent
metaphors such as metamorphosis, is constantly probing and
sceptical, a set of frameworks each tried as a possible solution
to experience from which entire, literal belief is provisionally
withheld. In this way they resemble, for instance, Donne's

mathematics and theology: not the beliefs that the poetry states so much as a series of lenses through which experience is tested in the project of inquiry the poetry embodies.

For all these reasons, *Les Amours de Cassandre* seems a text that remains very relevant to central contemporary concerns, such as current thought about the nature of human identity and the workings of the brain to manufacture or simulate it, and the literature and philosophy that seek to depict and help to form it. Modern ideas from neurology and psychology, and their philosophical consequences in theories of mind and language, seem now to be creating some form of convergence, in spirit though not in substance, with some of the complex and subtle ideas of the world and human nature current during the Renaissance. *Les Amours de Cassandre* does not have the feel of a text exhumed from a world entirely departed: it is a report on the experience of being human by a great poet whose mind on a deep level is far from alien to our own. The local strangeness can be overcome.

The Total Effect

The result of the richness of tones referred to above is that *Les Amours de Cassandre* is far from being a long and repetitive sequence of self-contained love poems each limited to the meaning expressly stated in it. Likewise, it is not a *roman à clef* or a love story sadly deprived of the clarity and sequential logic of the novella. It may, on first sight, be repetitive: there is a long sequence of poems whose central subject matter is the same, a number of tropes, images and formulations that occur again and again, and a standard Petrarchan paradigm familiar to all. Essentially, taken one by one, the sonnets are a series of brief sketches of a relationship perceived by one of its participants: encounters, thoughts, moments, speeches, emotional states. However, as we get to grips with the strategies being used in the totality that gradually emerges, we can see how each succeeding formulation is provisional and liable to be contradicted, reproducing the daily experience of the emotion depicted:

certain thoughts, ideas and facts rotate in an obsessive planetary system and are unavoidably and compulsively present while at the same time constantly forming new alignments and meanings, new configurations and potential applications in the minutiae of the day to day and the changing weather of the mind. The total, cumulative result is closer to the depiction of an obsessive love to be found, for instance, in the work of a novelist such as Proust than in a collection of unrelated amorous lyrics.

Repetition here therefore depicts a psychological truth, as does the exaggeration and heightening of emotion. They are not failures of imagination or perspective: they show the overwhelming nature of the experience of love and depict how in that crucible perspective and logic can be lost: how we self-dramatise, how we over-react, we repeat obsessively, we return compulsively to certain *idées fixes*; we look in books and to the arts for evidence of fellow sufferers, examples, survivors' stories, comparators; we question our perceptions, our experience and our deductions; we lie awake obsessively playing out scenes and scenarios in our minds – the many ways in which we are brought face to face with how we function as human beings when the comfortable self-delusions of everyday consciousness are temporarily stripped away.

Ronsard's achievement is to manipulate his different registers and paradigms using such wit, control and expressiveness that the result is a poetry that has not only an immediate aesthetic and emotional impact in its individual poems but also a rich intellectual impact in its cumulative form. It is a poetry loaded with information, of many kinds and on many levels, each piece of which adds another component to a rich and complex work of art. The display of conscious art in the sequence comes even more clearly into focus in the Elegies with which later editions conclude – much lighter and more ironical, worldly even, in tone, they pull back from the febrile world created in the sonnets and reveal more of the literary, political and biographical background amidst which they were written. Their effect is almost like that moment in some films when heightened colours return to normal and we are back in the world of the everyday, and thus understand and can acknowledge the emphases and dislocations we have just left behind.

The overall result is a great, though not flawless, sonnet sequence. Not every component poem is a masterpiece: Ronsard is an endlessly resourceful, careful, technically brilliant poet and a constant reviser, but he appears to be one of those poets who takes the view that once the poem is written it has an autonomous existence, for better or worse, and while it can be improved, sometimes over many versions and many years, a total recasting is a new poem entirely. As a result, sometimes the effect is similar to that of a sketchbook in which the artist, rather than rework and rework one sketch, reaches a point of relative satisfaction with it, then turns the page and makes another. That is Ronsard's style: he is a copious and fluent writer who constantly forms a poem then moves on. Poetry seemed to come to him with great facility, although the work he put into it is never to be underestimated. This is a man, however, who dictated his final poems, and great poems at that, on his deathbed: one for whom poetry was second nature. That for such a writer, in a work of such range and extent, there are imperfections seems therefore to be little more than an automatic consequence, the price to be paid for the inventiveness and variety his approach offers.

A word or two should be said about the style and the texture of the verse in *Les Amours de Cassandre*. The first thing that immediately strikes the reader is the quality of craftsmanship: even when dealing with arcane topics and indulging his love for neologisms (this is poetry that falls before, and runs entirely counter to, the purifying and pruning of the French language later championed by such writers as Malherbe), Ronsard is almost always natural, unforced and graceful. The verse moves deftly and with a lightness that frequently belies the weight of its content. Very rarely is there either padding to get to the end of a line or unseemly clutter within it, and few words strike one as owing their selection solely to rhyme or rhythm. Words speak to the ear with a natural intonation and a sense of the breath of the poet, and the sonnet's intrinsic textures and progressions are controlled masterfully: the rhetorical shaping of the language falls into the music of the verse with a rightness that frequently gives a sense of inevitability, and attunes the ear to any intentional disruptions of that pattern. There is a live and immediate sense of a speaker shaping the material in the moment rather than of a voice borrowing pre-existing music.

Similarly, the material is shaped within the sonnet form so as to capitalise upon its structures of repetition and return, its pauses and disjunctions, rather than in a way that struggles with them. When the form is subverted or wrenched one can have the confidence that this is an intentional effect and not the result of ineptitude. These sonnets have numerous rhetorical shapes and internal melodies, a multitude of voices.

Ronsard, English and the English Tradition

Ronsard is a poet who has never yet fully gelled with the English-speaking world. His international fame during his life-time extended as far as Britain (gifts and praises came to him from all over Europe, including from Mary Queen of Scots and Elizabeth I of England), but did not result in any true roots being struck here. Spenser, the English poet whose career has the most superficial resemblances to that of Ronsard (although the differences between are them are vast), translated Ronsard's friend, colleague and rival Du Bellay at length, but while he clearly read Ronsard, and appears to have borrowed his influence in a few passages, he seems to have attempted no similar extended translation of him.

Ronsard's work was clearly an influence on Sidney in *Astrophil and Stella* and, both directly and through Sidney, on the English sonneteers as a whole. The nearest equivalent in English of *Les Amours de Cassandre* would probably be Sidney's *Astrophil and Stella*, rather than (for instance) Spenser's *Amoretti*. However, the English sonnet after Sidney, in Shakespeare and his contemporaries and followers, frequently has significantly, if subtly, different characteristics of organisation and tone from those to be found in *Les Amours de Cassandre*. Ronsard here adopts the 'Petrarchan' model of the sonnet transmitted from the Italian originators of the form, with a few variants. This creates a poem in two distinct formal parts, an octet of the first eight lines and then a sestet of the concluding six, with the octet rhyming ABBA ABBA, and the sestet either rhyming CCD EED or showing some variant of that pattern. In English the sonnet, once it had been fully domesticated, fell most frequently into a form that reflected the comparative paucity of rhymes in the language by using, typically, the 'Shakespearean' form of three quatrains building to the concluding epigrammatic couplet or similar constructions. There are also other 'hybrid' forms, such as that developed by Spenser.

The resulting rhetorical structures and strategies adopted, and the tone communicated to the poetry, will inevitably diverge where the formal changes are so marked, even where there is a shared underlying tradition. For instance, in the characteristic English form of the sonnet, the separation between the content of octet and sestet becomes less pronounced or disappears altogether where that division ceases to have any formal relevance, and on occasions is replaced by a separation between the content of the quatrains and the concluding couplet. A lower intensity in the linkage between lines by rhyme opens out the form by releasing it from the necessity always to 'double back' on itself, particularly in the octet. Three quatrains can supply three consecutive propositions and a couplet a neat or paradoxical conclusion. The ways in which the different formal configurations then embody the material used in them, and affect the very nature and handling of that material, cause differences that can outweigh what otherwise appear to be high levels of similarity in subject matter, vocabulary and attitude.

Les Amours de Cassandre therefore reads in a different way, both in its individual poems and in its totality, to the well-known English sonnet sequences such as those by Shakespeare, Drayton, Daniel or Spenser. To attempt to generalise as to the precise nature of that difference in a short introduction such as this is fraught with all the dangers of over-simplification. One example of the difference might however be suggested as follows. Where the 'classic' English sonnet will often tend towards being a self-contained, authoritative statement, even where that is a statement of irresolution or paradox, the Ronsard sonnet is frequently more provisional and investigatory, more open to an exploratory beginning and an ambiguous or a tentative resolution. On the level of the sequence as a whole, *Les Amours de Cassandre* builds itself out of its individual poems, each of which is in itself true to the moment and sincere in its assertions but proves ultimately to be provisional, to form a picture that emerges in a cumulative and associative way, whereas the English sequences typically map out a more distinct and linear narrative or an intellectual and emotional progress by a series of individual attempts at rhetorical finality.

Ronsard's work as a whole is vast and, in view of its quality and the widely held view that it represents the finest non-dramatic body of poetry in French prior to the nineteenth century, the access routes made into it by English translation are surprisingly few. There have been famous translations of individual Ronsard poems by major poets such as Keats, Yeats (although his deservedly famous version of a Ronsard poem, 'When you are old and grey and full of sleep', is more an adaptation than a translation), and Sylvia Plath. There have also been contemporary translations of selections from the poetry published over recent years in major imprints, so the position is by no means one of total neglect, but Ronsard remains a writer insufficiently known in English.

A few translations of individual poems from *Les Amours de Cassandre* have appeared over the years, some in the Elizabethan era by Thomas Lodge. It is perhaps symptomatic of Ronsard's near invisibility in English-speaking cultures that in a comparatively recent Everyman edition where a couple of these translations appear as selections (sonnets 34 and 35 from Lodge's *Phillis*) they are not identified in the annotation as translations. That, however, is entirely understandable: there does not seem to have been a full translation of the *Amours de Cassandre* into English before. Hopefully that fact in itself is justification enough for the present translation.

The Present Translation

In this translation I started from the position that the sonnet is so structured and historically hallowed a form that a poem written in it adopts and adapts not only the external shape but also the patterns of thought imposed by it. For that reason, if it is to be translated into verse rather than prose, it can only be rendered in a similar sonnet configuration. That decision having been made, translating sonnets into sonnets necessarily involves sacrifices to the exigencies of the form. In particular, I have reproduced in each case the full form, which as stated above is a series of variations of the Petrarchan sonnet, in which the line is a decasyllable rather than the alexandrine used both by the later Ronsard and others as the standard pattern for the French sonnet. I have not sought to simplify rhyme schemes but have always reproduced those of the original: while there are inevitably some casualties in this approach, the form is crucial to the sense of movement, the pacing and breath, of a Ronsard sonnet, even to its argument, and to divide it too clearly in a way not authorised by the original seemed unjustifiable.

Ronsard's original publication of *Les Amours de Cassandre* was accompanied by musical settings, five options to which any sonnet could be sung. While it would entirely overstate the case to suggest that these poems are 'words for music', this is suggestive of the extent to which these issues of pacing and breath are central to the form, and I have tried to retain them as far as possible. The alternation of masculine and feminine rhymes adopted by Ronsard is one aspect I have not tried to reproduce, for reasons dictated by the comical effect too soon encountered in English as well as those of difficulty. The rhymes I have used will be seen to belong frequently to various species of half-rhyme or approximate rhyme: apart from the greater number of options that enables, it also accords with contemporary practice and, given the relative frequency of rhymes between French and English, does not in my view unduly distort the music of the verse when transposed into English.

I have tried to remain essentially faithful to the literal meaning of the original, although it may be that on occasions I have been more accurate to my own misapprehensions of the meaning: Ronsard's sense is sometimes ambiguous and hard to decipher, even for his contemporaries, hence the Muret annotations of 1553. I have had to recognise that this desire for accuracy is an ultimately unattainable object at the same time as it entails many sacrifices of elegance. A verse translation cannot strive for the analytical exactness available to a prose version.

I have done very little real modernisation of the text, and have confined what I have done to those places where without such modernisation I felt that meaning would be distorted or immediacy lost. For instance, when dealing with Ronsard's frequent references to classical mythology, I have sometimes used some latitude to gloss silently some of the references, avoid a few periphrastic namings of mythological characters, and to avoid some wordings I thought no longer worked in an English version. On the whole, however, it is surprising how little requires this kind of treatment: even in fairly arcane areas of thought, the expressions Ronsard uses remain thoroughly comprehensible. Typically, grand statements need little adaptation, whereas the less considered, intimate or vernacular moments can present more difficulty. It is almost as if in language the large denominations remain current while the small change passes quickly out of circulation.

An example of this arises in the context of certain endearments or oblique references to Cassandra, where my departures from Ronsard's original wording are not cases of trying to import contemporary sexual mores into poetry written in the sixteenth century so much as trying to avoid the connotations those contemporary mores have imprinted in today's language when they would import meanings that are not there in the original. On some occasions, for instance, Ronsard addresses Cassandra as his 'mistress': not a word that works now, unless its judgemental modern undertones fit the context. Or there are times where Ronsard addresses or refers to Cassandra in the third person as a 'nymph', and to reproduce this directly not only brings in modern English a sense of jarring archaism but also, in so far as there is any modern connotation, brings the wrong, Nabokovian one. (I have retained one use of the word where Ronsard playfully addresses Cassandra in that way: I felt that survived.) There are a few changes of that kind, judgement calls that are dictated by my bearing always in mind that the object of the exercise is a contemporary English version that can be read with pleasure. My aim in making such changes was not to alter or obscure any element that made a significant contribution to the meaning or tone of the poetry but to prevent that meaning or tone from being obscured by literalism.

These original poems contain little padding: Ronsard packs the line and the poem with information of many kinds, and my main objective throughout has been to preserve as much of that information as I can throughout the translation, taking the approach that this poetry will always have a real element of 'strangeness' to a contemporary Anglophone reader that is for many part of its attraction, and that even where that strangeness is an obstacle to the reader, it will not be improved by smoothing every unfamiliar or jarring element into the clichés of our time. In trying at the same time however to write a contemporary language I am aware that I may have fallen between incompatible objectives: that is the risk translation always entails, and negotiating that risk as best as one can is part of the pleasure and challenge of doing it.

There is a particular difficulty in rendering consistently certain recurring words and concepts, especially where the breadth of meanings such a word can encompass in French is not matched by any of its English equivalents. It seems clear that Ronsard's repetitions and references of this kind from poem to poem are as deliberate as such repetitions are within a poem, but, while I have done what I can to reproduce this, I have been unable to remain entirely consistent, both for reasons of localised meaning and from requirements of form. Such words include such constant companions as *doux/douce*, which I have usually translated as 'sweet', that being the most frequently serviceable English alternative; *langueur*, where I have used 'weakness', or 'wasting', as well as 'pining', even occasionally 'languidness' or 'languor'; and *beau/bel/belle*, whose monosyllable seems designed by some cruel lexical deity to torture any metrical translator into English.

The result is the inevitable hybrid familiar to all who read translations of this kind: something that would be both more accurate and more elegant if it could, the result of a constant process of compromise and an endless sequence of trade-offs. My hope for what ultimately emerges, however, is that it provides a sequence of poems in English that exists in its own right, for all its imperfections, while giving a real flavour of what a great poet Ronsard is, bringing into English something of Ronsard's unique tone and personality as a writer, and reflecting some of his contribution to a poetic form whose fascination seems never to have disappeared throughout all the revolutions of literary fashion.

My translation is based on the final text established by Ronsard and published with his authority, that of 1584. Other editions are available, including editions that show Ronsard's 'first thoughts', and there is much interest to be derived from reviewing the changes from the 1550s to the 1580s. Many of these changes are just the tidying of a careful craftsman, others go deeper: a full account and analysis of all of them would be a topic for a PhD thesis (and no doubt has been). However, given the nature of Ronsard as a writer and the clear sense he had of an oeuvre that as it progressed formed an organic whole, I have gone with his final thoughts. That is the approach taken both by the editors of the appropriately named Bibliothèque de la Pléiade standard edition of Ronsard's works, and in the Gallimard edition of the sonnet cycles, entitled *Les Amours*, where the text is presented in a modernised orthography established by Albert-Marie Schmidt in 1964; and it seems to be the best solution, not least because it also helps to place *Les Amours de Cassandre* amongst the other sonnet sequences, and then within the oeuvre as a whole.

CASSANDRA

I

Whoever wants to see how Love can tame
My soul, attack me, strut his victories,
And reignite a heart he means to freeze,
And how he makes a trophy of my shame;

Whoever wants to see rash youth in vain
Pursuit of what will cause it miseries,
Come read this book: watch me in this disease
Neither my Goddess nor my God will name.

And know that love has neither right nor reason,
Gently beguiles and royally imprisons,
Raises false hope and feeds us on fresh air;

And know the self-delusion of a fool
So far astray he lets a blind boy school
His steps, and a mere infant domineer.

II

Nature, giving Cassandra's beauty powers
To rule with sweetness the most rebel minds,
Composed her from a hundred novel kinds
Of loveliness held back a thousand years.

From all that Love the bird broods over, rears
Beneath his wings in loveliest Heaven's bounds,
Nature condensed immortal grace, the glance
Of those fine eyes that move the Gods to tears.

3

Scarcely had she descended out of Heaven
When first I saw her, and my soul was riven
To madness for her: Love's transfixing dart

Diffused her beauty through my every vein,
So all my other pleasures feel like pain,
And to adore this portrait's all I've got.

III

From there, between the rays of that twin fire
He tends, I saw Love drawing back his bow,
And in my heart that flame began to glow
That sears the coldest marrow with desire:

Next to my Lady's eyes, fine golden wire,
Covered in flowers, snared me, parted in two,
Clustered in curls that frame her face and flow
In ravelled waves to bind my soul to her.

What could I do? The Archer was so sweet,
So sweet his fire, so sweet each golden knot –
In these bonds I forget myself at last.

Still I forget without anxiety,
So sweetly the sweet Archer pierces me,
Fire burns me and this spun gold holds me fast.

IV

Warrior Cassandra, I am not some vicious
Myrmidon or Dolopean from the wars,[1]
Nor yet that Archer whose lethal bolt caused
Your brother's death[2] and burned your towers to ashes.

No army sets sail with the tide that rushes
From Aulis[3] to enslave you to my cause,
And look, beneath your ramparts, no fleet moors
Its thousand ships to take you in its clutches.

Me? I'm just Coroebus,[4] the simpleton
Whose heart takes mortal wounds and yet lives on,
Struck not by Greek Peneleos, but by

A little sharp-shooter whose hundred darts
Flew in a single volley through my eye,
When recklessly he shot me through the heart.

1 Classical mythology: Myrmidons and Dolopeans are Greek troops at the
   siege of Troy.
2 Classical mythology: Cassandra's brother, Paris, was killed by the archer
   Philoctetes.
3 Classical mythology: Aulis is the port from which the Greek fleet sailed to
   Troy.
4 Classical mythology: Coroebus was a Phrygian warrior who came to the
   Trojan War out of love for Cassandra and was killed there by the Greek
   warrior Peneleos.

V

I try comparisons: sun I adore,
And, there, that other sun. That with its eyes
Kindles, ignites, illuminates the skies,
This makes our France's lustre shine the more.

The whole freight of the box Pandora[1] bore,
All elements, all stars, all deities,
And all the best that Nature could devise
Decked her I honour out in their allure.

Ha! I'd have been too happy had cruel fate
Not walled behind an adamantine gate
So chaste a heart, beneath so fair a face,

And had my heart, ripped from my chest, not mixed
In my betrayal, just to be transfixed,
And riveted with fire into her ice!

1 Classical mythology: Pandora was the first woman, who was given by the
   gods an array of divine and alluring gifts (see XXXII). Zeus also gave her a
   box containing all the world's evils, which she opened out of curiosity,
   setting them free throughout the world, leaving only hope behind. The refer-
   ence here, however, seems to be more to the gifts conferred on Pandora by
   the gods than to the evils in the box.

VI

Those golden fetters, that vermilion mouth,
Where lilies, roses and carnations dwell,
Those eyebrows, crescent moons set parallel,
That cheek, like Dawn in her first flush of youth;

Those hands, that neck, that brow, that ear's whorled groove,
Those breasts like ripe green buds that strain and swell,
Those eyes, twin scintillating stars whose spell
Makes souls tremble in wonder as they move,

6

All wove their bonds together, built a nest
So fertile Love could brood within my chest
The eggs he swelled with, hatch them in my blood.

How can I live save in a wasting state,
Now I find this ever-renewing brood
Of Cupids hatched and fledging in my heart?

VII

For all it pleases you to set on fire
My heart, this faithful heart in which you reign,
Not with a love's, but with a Fury's flame
Cruelly consuming these bones as they sear,

Wrongs others find too bitter can inspire
Sweetness in my mouth, so it's not my aim
To make complaints: I prize life to the same
Extent as my life pleases you, no higher.

But, Lady, if Heaven gave me birth to be
Your victim, let me give my loyalty,
Not my poor soul, for sacrificial meat.

And you should let my offering do you good,
Not simply immolate itself in blood,
And burn alive there at your beauty's feet.

VIII

When it delights my eye to gaze on you
Your eye has power to discharge a shock
That strikes me and transfixes me to rock,
Like petrifying Medusa's[1] glances do;

If, serving you with lyre in hand to show
Your glory, I lack subtle art to pluck
An instrument fit only for Petrarch,
Your cruelty (it confesses) made it so.

But what have I said? Though a rock may hold
Me walled inside, I still would not make bold
To blame you, when your anger's flames hold terrors –

Lest my poor head is battered in the assault
Of your eyes' fire, as mountains in Epirus[2]
Are battered by the heavens' thunderbolt.

1 Classical mythology: Medusa was a Gorgon whose hair was made up of
   writhing snakes and whose look turned those who saw it to stone.
2 Epirus in Greece was a mountainous region reputed to be prone to light-
   ning.

IX

The deepest thicket in a pathless wood,
The craggiest peak where savage mountains soar,
The loneliest place on a deserted shore,
The stillest caves' unnerving solitude,

So soothe my voice, comfort my sighs I could –
Only there, where most secret shades obscure
My solitude – feel love's rage find some cure,
Rage maddening the greenest months I've had.

And there I throw myself down on hard ground,
And take the portrait that I keep around
My heart, my only anodyne for pain;

One glance – the beauties Denisot[1] portrays
Unleash the thousand metamorphoses
I feel roll through each time I look again.

1   Nicholas Denisot (1515–59) was a painter and poet.

X

Love feeds such an Ambrosia to me
No envy in this world can make me prize
That liquor which, at Ocean's[1] banquet, tries
The Father of the Gods' sobriety.

The girl who captivates my liberty,
Imprisoning my heart within her eyes,
Consoles my hunger with fruit of such price
No other taste ignites my fantasy.

I never tire of gulping it down, so
The joys of one mutating thought renew
My appetite that night and day revives;

And if gall didn't bear its bitter part
To taint the honey sweetness in my heart,
To be a god with gods would not entice.

1   Classical mythology: Ocean is one of the Titans, the god of the river that
surrounds the world. The reference is to the banquet he held for Zeus.

XI

Ah, Traitor Love, give me peace, give me truce,
Or choose a sturdier arrow for your bow,
Cut off my life, bring death to lay me low;
Death is the sweeter the swifter it goes.

The torments growing in my mind infuse
My blood and gnaw the soul of me right through,
And destine me like Ixion[1] below,
Whose punishment eternally ensues.

What should I do? Love leads me such a round,
So in command, I daren't hope for safe ground,
Only a slow decline that wastes by stealth.

And since my God won't help and just stands by,
My choice to save myself would be to die,
And so to kill death by my death itself.

1   Classical mythology: Ixion fell in love with Hera and tried to rape her. His punishment was to be tied to a wheel of fire in the underworld.

XII

I hope and fear, keep silent and cry out;
Sometimes I'm ice, sometimes a raging fire;
Admiring all, while nothing makes me care;
I loose my collar, button to the throat.

Nothing contents me but what doesn't suit;
I'm brave, yet my heart quails, bids me retire;
My hope descends, my courage rises higher;
I dread Love's power, defying him to shoot.

The more I try, the more I misbehave;
I love my freedom, yearn to be a slave;
Desiring all, one longing fills my head.

I'm a Prometheus[1] to passion's beak:
I dare, I want, I strive, I'm still too weak,
That Fate[2] weaves life for me from such black thread.

1 Classical mythology: Prometheus, the Titan, stole fire from heaven and gave
   it to humankind. As a punishment he was transfixed to a rock, and a vulture
   came each day to peck out his liver (which re-grew after each attack).
2 Classical mythology: the Fate referred to is one of the Three Fates who spun,
   wove and then cut the thread of each person's life.

XIII

For loving your eyes' sunshine to excess,
And not for stealing their divine spark, see
Love drives his thousand magnets into me
To nail me to your rock, hard-heartedness.

No eagle, but cruel care, making his mess,
Clawing this wound that bleeds eternally,
Devours my heart; yet that god makes no plea
To my Lady, to soothe me in distress.

But out of hundreds of pains that engulf
Me nailed, transfixed here to your hard resolve,
The cruellest would seem sweetest, if, just once,

I hoped to see, after long ages passed,
The Hercules[1] of your grace come at last,
Just to untie the least one of my bonds.

1 Classical mythology: Hercules was a demi-god of legendary strength, famed
   for a number of heroic exploits including the 'twelve labours'. Hercules
   freed Prometheus (see note to XII) from his torments, shooting the eagle that
   came to devour his liver.

XIV

When first my eyes met yours, such a planet reigned
That, since, I find no joy in anything
Save when, in solitude, I sigh and sing,
'My brown-haired beauty, come and ease my pain.'

O freedom, how I wish you'd come again,
And rue the day I saw you vanishing,
To leave me without hope, a wretched thing,
Tormented in the false hopes that remain.

The twenty-first of April now is past:
A year has gone by since I came at last
Into this prison, where the Cupids cry;

And yet my fetters are so strong I see
There's no way out, there's no escape for me,
Unless in death all my deaths come to die.

XV

Ah, Homer's Graces[1] had it right, who found
Swift action's true comparison in thought,
That far outflies Bellerophon's winged horse[2]
That bore him off to cut Chimaera down!

The fleeting galleon that beats around
From sea to sea's no faster in its course;
Nor could Renown, its true and false reports
Winging it through the fields, run thought to ground.

The North Wind, Boreas, who knows no rest,
Imagined my thought naturally blessed
That soars through Heaven, dives through seas and scours

The fields, fired, like Zethes the Argonaut,[3]
With energy, to fly after my heart,
Which now a Harpy gleefully devours.

1 Classical mythology: the Graces, usually three in number, were goddesses
   of creativity, charm and beauty, named Aglaia, Euphrosyne and Thalia.
2 Classical mythology: Bellerophon rode Pegasus the winged horse, and the
   Chimaera was a monster he killed.
3 Classical mythology: Zethes was one of the Boreads, children of Boreas, who
   helped to drive the winged monsters, the Harpies, away from Phineus
   during the voyage of the Argonauts. The Harpies tormented Phineus by
   stealing and polluting his food.

XVI

I want to let this pain I'm feeling fly
Through France, swifter than a bolt from a bow;
I want to stop my ears with honey, so,
Deaf to my Siren's voice,[1] I can pass by.

I want to make a fountain of each eye,
My heart a fire, my head a rock, my slow
Sad feet a tree trunk, so I'll never go
Back to her beauty's cruel humanity.

I want to change my thoughts to birds, these sighs
I whisper to new Zephyrs that will rise
To vent through all the world my sad complaint.

I want my pallor, by the banks of the Loir,[2]
To bring into the world a new pale flower
For my name and my suffering to paint.[3]

1 Classical mythology: the Sirens lured sailors to shipwreck with the sweet-
   ness of their songs: see the *Odyssey*, Book XII.
2 The Loir was the river near Ronsard's home in the Vendôme region – not
   the more famous Loire.
3 There is a reference here to a device used by the Ronsard family as a possible
   derivation of their name, the 'ronce' (a bramble or bramble flower) '(qui)
   ard' (which burns).

13

XVII

Destiny wants my soul to be their home –
Her eye, her hand, her loosened mane of hair –
Which burned, grasped, bound me with such brutal power
That, seared, clasped, tangled, I must feel death come.

The fire, grasp, snare that every hour resume
Charring, compressing, knotting my love, steer
Me, sacrificed at my half-soul's feet there,
Towards a better life via death's doom.

Eye, hand and hair, who burn up, who oppress
And coil around my heart that you possess
Within the labyrinth your windings spread,

Why can't I speak with Ovid's golden tongue?
Eye, you would be a fine star in my song;
Hand, a fine lily; hair, a fine silk thread.

XVIII

A youthful beauty, of just fifteen years;[1]
A golden mass of hair in ringlet curls;
A rose-petal complexion, like a girl's;
A laugh that lifts my soul into the stars;

A virtue worth the beauty that it wears;
A snow-white neck, a milk-white throat, a soul's
Maturity in flesh time still unfurls;
A divine beauty a human Lady shares;

An eye with power to turn night into day;
A gentle hand, to drive my cares away,
Whose fingers hold my life locked in its prison;

14

Now with a sweetly fashioned song, and then
Sometimes a smile, sometimes a groan of pain –
These are the sorcerers that charmed my reason.

1 This sonnet refers to Cassandra's age at the time of Ronsard's first meeting
with her in 1545, some years before the majority of the sonnets in this
sequence appear to have been written. See Introduction for a discussion of
the ordering of the sonnets.

XIX

'Before their time, your temples will bloom white,
Your end is a few numbered days away;
Before the night falls, time will close your day,
Your mind that hope betrayed shrink as it dies;

Your poems will desiccate in my dry eyes,
Your ruin show my destiny the way,
For I was born to lead the poets astray,
And all posterity will mock your sighs.

You'll be a folk-tale fool, mocked through the land,
Building uncertainty in shifting sand,
Painting the skies with your vain fantasy!'

That's what the girl who drives me mad once said.
Then, as her witness, Heaven flashed overhead,
And that deft omen wasn't lost on me.

XX

I wish I could transmute, ripening through yellow
To fall in golden rain showers, drop by drop
Into my beautiful Cassandra's lap
While sleep insinuates across her pillow.

I wish I could transform, to foam and bellow,
A white bull; bend my back, set her on top,
When she, a flower, in April goes to crop
A thousand flowers through the freshest meadow.[1]

I wish, to pacify this suffering,
I was Narcissus,[2] she a mountain spring,
To plunge into her, for one sweet night's stay;

And I could wish that night could last forever
Into eternity, and that Dawn never
Might reignite to wake me with the day.

1 Classical mythology: the references are to Zeus's metamorphoses into a
  golden rain to seduce Danaë and into a bull to abduct Europa.
2 Classical mythology: Narcissus was a beautiful youth who fell in love with
  his reflection in a pool and pined to death for it.

XXI

Let Love sound out my heart, fathom my soul,
Love, who knows well how I have just one aim:
He'll find that passion's all-devouring flame
Roars through my veins, past hope, beyond control.

God, how I love her! Is it possible
For any heart in this world to contain
Such yearning for perfection's beauty, the pain
That scars so deep a wound into my soul?

The black horse that my Queen, my Reason, rides,
Seduced to follow paths where my flesh guides,
Has wandered false trails so far from its way,

That my great fear's that if the good white horse
Can't check her mad career, direct her course
Back to the yoke, Reason will go astray.[1]

1 Neo-Platonism: the *Phaedra* of Plato contains allusions to the Queen, Reason, the black horse she rides, which represents the sensual impulses and the irrational desires, and the white horse, which represents moral impulses and the aspiration towards the good.

XXII

To think one thought hundreds, hundreds of times,
Strip my heart naked to two lovely eyes,
Always drink bitterness down to the lees,
Feed always on the bitterest extremes;

To show a soul, a face, sick pallor shames;
To bend her rigour less the more my sighs;
To die of heartache, hide my weaknesses;
To let another's will dictate my aims;

In brief resentment, iron fidelity,
To love, more than myself, my enemy;
Daub with a thousand masks my face beneath;

To want to cry, yet dare not gasp for air;
To live in hope and perish in despair:
These are the surest omens of my death.

XXIII

All this bright coral, this marble that sighs,
This ebony, an eyebrow's ornament,
This alabaster's vaulted monument,
These sapphires, jaspers and these porphyries,

These diamonds, rubies, that a Zephyr's breeze
Inspires with life as its sweet sighs relent,
These pinks, these roses, this fine gold's rich tint
Where gold itself reflects on its own price,

Stir such profound emotion in my soul
My mind has space for nothing else at all
Beside, Belleau,[1] their beauty I adore;

And that sweet pleasure that can never go
Away – to dream of them, to think them through,
Then dream of them and think them through once more.

1   Rémy Belleau (1528–77) was one of the poets of La Brigade (La Pléiade).

XXIV

Your eyes are kind: I see you promise there
The gift I'd lack the insolence to seek;
Yet I fear the inheritance they take
From King Laomedon,[1] your ancestor.

Their double torch ignites me: in their flare
Hope clasped my mind, enticing me to make
Predictions their delusive grace will break,
That some reward might come for all my care.

Only your mouth speaks out, scares me: that mouth,
That makes you a true Prophetess, sings truth
In recantation of your loving eyes.

That's how I live, that's how I die: in doubt.
One calls me back, the other kicks me out;
So from one source my joy and sadness rise.

1   Classical mythology: Laomedon was a Trojan king, father of Priam (and so
    Cassandra's grandfather), famous for breaking his word.

XXV

That pair of brown eyes, my life's guiding lights,
That dazzle mine in the clear beams they shed,
Enslaved the freedom of my youth and read
Its sentence: servitude, with no respite.

Your brown eyes snatched my reason from me quite:
If there was any place Love stopped me dead,
No other beauty ever turned my head:
They were my sole desire, my sole delight.

My master plagues me with no other gall;
No other thoughts can lodge in me at all;
No other fire can set my Muse ablaze.

My hand can learn to write no other name;
My paper takes no ink until I stain
It with their beauty that my soul obeys.

XXVI

Sooner the ballet of these scattered stars
Will tire, and waves will cease to fret the sea;
Sooner the wandering sun forget to flee
And run its circuits round this earth of ours;

Sooner the walls of Heaven will split apart,
The world collapse to formless entropy,
Than any blonde girl make a slave of me
Or green-eyed woman captivate my heart.

O beautiful brown eye my soul obeys,
Your flame's set me so utterly ablaze
That no green eye can claim me for its own!

Your power's so strong, if my skin's young or wears
Time's wrinkles, if my soul's set loose, as ideas
I'll love them still: heart's suns, fine eyes of brown.

XXVII

I've tried a thousand, many thousand times
To sound out on the nerve-strings of my lyre
And write down, darkening paper by the quire,
The name Love's rooted in this heart of mine.

All of a sudden, terror claws my mind:
Her beautiful name, my mind's martyr's pyre,
Shocks me out of myself, and in my dire
Torment a hundred furies chase behind.

I'm like the Pythoness[1] when she's possessed,
Who stammers, lost for words in mindlessness
Beneath the fierce god who bewilders her.

20

And love so grips me and possesses me
That, maddened, I can only gape to see
Myself made speechless, my voice disappear.

1 Classical mythology: the Pythoness was the prophetic Sibyl of Delphi who
   spoke verses inspired by Apollo when possessed by the god.

XXVIII

Unjust Love, sparking rage on every side,
What can a heart that's subject to your power
Do, when you choose our senses to unmoor
Our reason, that's our courage's sole guide?

I can't see meadow, flower, cave, riverside,
Field, rock or wood, the current of the Loir,[1]
Without seeing painted shadows I think are
That beauty that caught and enslaved my pride.

Now morphed to lightning flashing through the thunder,
A torrent or a tiger wild with hunger,
Love's fantasy leads them through night's pursuit.

But when in dreams I reach my hand to clasp
Fire, ship or torrent, they elude my grasp,
And I hold only void in place of truth.

1 For the Loir, see note to XVI.

XXIX

If I clasp to my heart a thousand pinks
And lilies, to entwine my arms around
More tightly than a vine, whose loving bond
Enclasps the loved branch in its thousand links;

If I'm no longer jaundiced by the stings
Of care, and pleasure in me holds its ground;
If I prefer night's shade to daylight's brand,
Divine dream, it's your grace gives me these wings.

I would pursue your flight into the skies,
But that portrait of her deludes my eyes,
Forever cheats my interrupted joy.

So just as I feel good, you flee me then,
Like lightning that just flashes in the pan,
Or like a cloud the rising winds destroy.

XXX

Divine Angel, who steep my wounds in balm,
Herald and go-between of deity,
From which of Heaven's gates did you slip free
To bathe the sufferings of my soul in calm?

You, when the night turns all my thoughts to flame,
It's you who pity my anxiety
And float into my arms, before my eye,
That simulacrum with my Lady's name.

Stay, Dream, stay with me just a moment longer!
Deceiver, wait till I can blunt the hunger
For that vain portrait that's devouring me.

22

I'm dying for her body. Grant I might,
If not in fact, in dream's facsimile,
Just hold it in my arms through one whole night.

XXXI

You light-winged Demons[1] who possess by right
Dominion over heaven and the earth,
Divine messengers through air God sends forth
To bring his secrets swiftly to the light;

Tell me (so may no sorcerer draw tight
His ring of fire around you), scouring our turf,
Haven't you seen that beauty – tell the truth –
That launches on me these cruel wars I fight?

If she by chance should see that you're down here,
You'll never make it back, free, to the air,
Her sweet power so sweetly can beguile;

Instead, she'll make slaves out of you, as once
She did of me, with beauty that transforms
With just one look, like a Medusa's[2] smile.

1 Neo-Platonism: Demons are spirits which are held to live in the air and to
   occupy a status between the human and the divine. See also note to
   CLXXVIII and note to CXCI.
2 Classical mythology: for Medusa, see note to VIII.

XXXII

When at her birth the Lady I adore
Brought all her beauties to adorn the skies,
Rhea's son[1] called all the gods to synthesise
A new Pandora,[2] as they had before.

Apollo did her honour then with four
Gifts: crystallised his sunbeams for her eyes,
Gave her the power of his melodies,
Then his prophetic and poetic lore.[3]

Mars gave to her all his ferocious cruelty;
Venus her laughter, Dione her beauty,
Peitho her voice, Ceres her rich profusion.[4]

Dawn's rosy fingers and her scattered hair,
Love's bow and Thetis' feet were given there;
Clio gave glory, Pallas gave her prudence.[5]

1 Classical mythology: Rhea's son is Zeus.
2 For Pandora see note to V.
3 Classical mythology: Apollo is the god of the sun, and of music, prophecy
   and poetry.
4 Classical mythology: Mars is the god of war, Venus goddess of love. Dione
   is the mother of Venus, Peitho the goddess of persuasion (or seduction),
   Ceres goddess of plenty.
5 Classical mythology: Thetis is the sea nymph who was mother of Achilles,
   Clio the Muse of history and Pallas goddess of wisdom.

XXXIII

I wouldn't be this folk-tale fool, deceived
To point a fable for posterity
If I could view the endgame rationally –
The final sentence your truth-telling leaves;

Chaste Prophetess, in whose heart pity grieves,
Cassandra, you often warn me, prophesy
How loving you will be the death of me –
But that's your tragedy: no one believes.

Harsh Destiny, who hides my death from view,
Compelling me to disbelieve in you,
Denies your oracles, just to confuse.

But then I see at last; and see the state
I'm in, and how you told the truth – too late –
I cannot shake my head free of this noose.

XXXIV

I'm grieved by thousands, thousands of these sighs
I drag to no avail from deep beneath
My heart, my heat gently infusing breath
Drenched in the tears distilled out of my eyes.

Then I'm grieved by her portrait's uselessness,
Mere shadow of what I adore, the truth
I follow, and those eyes' devouring teeth
Of flame that burn my heart in endless fires.

And yet, above all, I'm grieved by one thought
That all too often forces through my heart
The memory of beauty cruelty hones,

And one regret that bleaches me so clean
That I have no more blood left in my veins,
Strength in my sinews, marrow in my bones.

XXXV

Just let it come once: give me my revenge
On this thought that consumes my heart away,
And endlessly, a lion on its prey,
Devours what chokes there in its ruthless clinch.

Within time even time itself can change;
But that cruel beast that sucks life out of me,
Unwavering in its ferocity,
Settles on my heart for its only range.

It's true that while the day holds off the night
It's learned to curb its secret appetite,
And not to use my heart to flex its claws;

But when the evening holds day prisoner
The famished lion hunts again and there
Devours me all night with thousand-toothed jaws.

XXXVI

For that same grief that by Love's will I feel,
Like me, Phoebus Apollo,[1] you lamented
When lovestruck, exiled, you wandered and chanted
Divine song on Xanthus' banks, by Ilion's wall.[2]

You plucked your lyre, that once seduced them all:
And rivers, flowers and forests were enchanted,
But not that beauty your soul felt implanted
Within it, searing with corrosive gall.

26

There your pale face bleached colour from the flowers,
And rivulets grew swollen with your tears,
And there delusive hope kept you alive.

Love uses that same name to torture me,
Here, on the Loir's[3] banks, by Vendôme; and see –
I'm like a Phoenix my sufferings revive.

1 Classical mythology: Apollo was in love with Cassandra, who rejected him.
   See note to XXXII, and Introduction.
2 Classical mythology: the Xanthus was a river near Troy. Ilion is another
   name for Troy.
3 For the Loir, see note to XVI.

XXXVII

Atoms that fall through Chaos and traverse
All the coordinates of Space and Time,
Smashed into one another, intertwined,
And tangled bonds to build a universe.

Vexation, care and thought that never dares
To speak rained thick through my love's depths, combined
Their powers and forged a bond that has defined
The universe of love that my heart bears.

But if subjection to her golden hair,
Dawn-rosy fingers, ivory hands, should wear
Away with beauty's burden my life's thread,

Would I come back in water, earth or flame?
No – in a voice returned to earth to shame
My Lady's cruelty and ingratitude.

27

XXXVIII

Sweet was the arrow Love took from his quiver
To shoot at me, and sweet was the progression
I felt within me from the first infection
When I was struck by this bittersweet fever.

Sweet is her laughter and her voice that severs
My soul in rapture from my body's possession
When she sings, to her lute's sweet intercession,
This verse brought to life by her thumb's soft pressure.

Her voice distils such sweetness all around
You couldn't, if you didn't hear that sound,
Feel deep within your soul a new joy rise;

Without hearing her spellbind Love himself,
Laugh sweetly, sweetly sing, couldn't have felt –
How sweetly I could die there by her side.

XXXIX

Against my will, your eyes' spellbinding light
Overpowers my soul, and when I'd speak
Of how I'm dying, all you do is shake
With laughter – my disease is your delight.

At least, since nothing better will requite
My love, let me sigh as my life's strings break.
Your fine eyes' gross pride ties me to a stake,
Without your laughing at my careworn state.

To mock my lost health, laugh at all my pain,
Double my wretchedness with blithe disdain,
Hate one who loves you and live on the sounds

Of pain he utters; to break faith, breach duty –
Ah, can't you see how that, my cruel beauty,
Is to smear blood and murder on your hands?

XL

What beauty and what grace in flower I see
In your breast's vernal garden, whose curves swell
To raise two milk-white slopes the Loves[1] chose well
To serve them for their arrows' armoury.

A hundred things metamorphose in me
When I look on you, exquisite, twinned hill –
Or rather Spring's new rose-tree as you thrill
The morning with your roses' coquetry.

If Europa[2] had breasts this beautiful,
You wisely masqueraded as a bull,
When, Jupiter, you crossed the waves for your prize.

They don't call Heaven perfect on the ground
Of size, but like this breast, because it's round –
For it's in roundness true perfection lies.

1 Classical mythology: the Loves are the Erotes, gods in Venus/Aphrodite's
   retinue: Eros, Anteros, Himeros and Pothos.
2 Classical mythology: Zeus/Jupiter took the shape of a bull to steal away
   Europa.

XLI

When morning sees my sweet goddess unfurl
That coiling wealth of gold that spreads its shade
Down to her heels, and sees her twist and braid
Her lovely blonde hair in a hundred curls,

Then I compare her to the sea-foam girl[1]
Combing her long brown hair in a cascade
Or curling it in myriad swirls, conveyed
Across the oceans in her native shell.

For no mere woman yet born had her looks –
Her smile, her brow, the way she moves and walks,
Nor the twin stars that look out from her eyes.

No rocks, no waters, no woods sheltered yet
Nymphs who had hair that could play tricks like that,
Such lovely eyes, mouth of such loveliness.

1   Classical mythology: Venus/Aphrodite was the goddess born out of the sea-
foam.

XLII

Carnations scattered amongst lilies lose
In the comparison with her complexion;
Nor can spun gold surpass her hair's perfection,
Whether it's bound in sheaves or shaken loose.

From that mouth's coral vault she can produce
Sweet laughter that frees me from care's possession,
And where she walks, earth strives in emulation,
Meadows paint wildflowers where her footprint goes.

Her mouth breathes scents of amber and of musk.
What more can I say? When the plain is dusk
With thunderheads, and lightning cracks the skies,

30

I've seen her calm brow that the gods obey
Soothe Jupiter's fierce thunderbolts away,
And all the heavens bow down to her eyes.

XLIII

Now it's foreboding, now expectancy
That gathers in my heart and takes possession,
And neither wins in that war of attrition,
Equal alike in strength and fixity.

So filled with doubt or with complacency
And caught between hope, fear and mere suspicion,
For nothing better than vain self-delusion,
I promise my captive heart its liberty.

And will I never see the day before
I die, when I can pluck her springtime's flower,
Beneath whose shade my life's dark tale is told?

And will I never see myself enclasped
Love-weary in her arms, panting my last,
And dying that sweet death where I am held?

XLIV

I'd be Ixion and Tantalus,[1] consent
To the wheel, the hellish waters that beguile,
If, nakedness to nakedness, I'd feel
That beauty even angels can't transcend.

If that could be, Hell's final punishment
Would taste sweet to me: I could reconcile
Being a vulture's meal[2] or having to toil
To heave a rock uphill then redescend.[3]

31

To see or touch her breast's soft curvature
Could change love's destiny for me, secure
For me a Prince of Asia's regal lot.

Her kiss would make a demigod of me;
To quench this love's fire, breast to breast, would be
To make me an Ambrosia-eating god.

1 Classical mythology: for Ixion see note to XI. Tantalus was a king of Phrygia
punished in the underworld by having to stand in a pool of water under a
fruit tree. If he reached for fruit the branches would snatch it away; if he bent
to drink the water would recede from him.
2 Classical mythology: the reference is to Prometheus (see note to XII).
3 Classical mythology: the reference is to Sisyphus, condemned eternally to
roll a rock up to the top of a hill from which it then fell back down to the
bottom.

XLV

Love's killing me, but I won't raise my voice
To say what pleasing pain it is to die,
So great's my fear someone officiously
Treats the sweet agony behind my sighs.

It's true that, weak as I am, my desires
Look to the time renewed strength sets me free;
But I don't want my Lady to give me
My health back, martyrdom's so dear a prize.

So, weakness, hold your tongue; I sense the day
My mistress comes, after such long delay,
Seeing the wrong she does me by her pride,

And lets her sweetness take her rigour's place,
In imitation of God's holy grace,
That punishes and then sets blame aside.

XLVI

Lady, I would die for your loveliness:
That beautiful eye, on whose hook I'm held,
That gentle laughter, and that kiss that melts
Amber and musk, the kiss of a goddess.

I'd die for this tress of blonde hair, for this
Curvature of a breast too chaste to yield,
The strength this gentle hand has learned to wield
When one touch cures and brings fresh injuries.

Lady, I'd die for that complexion's dusk,
That voice, whose singing beauty so can clutch
My heart, and so alone dictate its mood;

And I would die in love's erotic fight,
Quenching this passion pent up in my blood
In your arms' tight embrace through one whole night.

XLVII

Lady, since that originating dart
Flew from your eyes bearing its charge of pain,
And black and white, the colours in them came
To overpower me and to breach my heart,

My soul felt its eternal burning start,
My heart's core harbouring that constant flame,
Love's beacon, where my weakness finds its aim,
The lovely fire that dries my body out.

All I do night and day is dream, and scour
This heart of mine I worry and devour,
Praying for Love to cut my life's last thread.

But he, who laughs at all my agony,
The more I call and ask him to my side,
The more he just plays deaf, and won't reply.

XLVIII

It's not her crowning gold whose curls entwine,
Nor this nor that mark dimpling in her smile,
Nor the soft contours of her throat's defile;
It's not the rounded dimple in her chin;

It isn't her beautiful eyes that mine
Elected rulers of my subject soul,
Nor the lovely breast out of which Cupid stole
To shoot the keenest bolt he could refine;

It's not her body where each Grace[1] resorts,
Nor beauties written in a thousand hearts
That have enslaved all my youthful affection.

It's just her mind, the sign our age was given,
Taking its share of all the gifts of heaven,
That makes me die just for its sheer perfection.

1 For the Graces, see note to XV.

XLIX

Love, Love, how beautiful my mistress is!
I could admire her eyes, to which I bow,
The grace, the hair that ornament her brow,
The scarlet mirror image of her lips.

But Love, Love, what of all her cruelties?
Sometimes from her disdain my sorrows grow,
Sometimes her spite incites my tears to flow,
Sometimes old wounds bleed new when she denies.

So just as her sweet beauty feeds my heart
With honey, so her cruelty imparts
Its bitter gall to turn my whole life sour;

This diet of contradictions I've been fed
Means sometimes I'm alive, sometimes I'm dead,
Just like the fate Castor and Pollux share.[1]

1 Classical mythology: Castor and Pollux were twin brothers whose immor-
tality was shared between the two in alternation as the constellation Gemini.

L

A hundred times a day my bewildered thoughts
Debate this thing called Love: what in the mind
Sustains it; how its bow draws; where it finds
Its place in our hearts; its essential cause.

I understand the influence of the stars,
How the sea flows out yet always rebounds,
And how the Whole contains all this world's ends:
Still Love alone eludes me, hides its laws.

I'm certain it's a god of a powerful race
That, changeable, will sometimes take its place
Within my heart, sometimes beat down my veins;

That naturally it never comes to good,
And that it bears a worthless-tasting fruit
Out of a tree whose branches groan with pains.

LI

Thousands – it's true – thousands and thousands more,
My warrior Cassandra, yearned for me
To leave you, and in tearing myself free
From your snares, choose to live bound by their law.

But my heart, mine no longer, has this flaw:
It couldn't hear anyone else's plea.
You are its Lady, and it would sooner die
Ten thousand deaths than be no longer yours.

So long as the rose blossoms on the thorn,
And fed by rising sap the Spring is born,
And red deer love the cover of green trees;

So long as love feeds on the tears we weep,
I'll always bear on my heart, graven deep,
Your name, your known worth and your loveliness.

LII

Before Love came to Chaos' waste, to prise
Open its womb that held the light of day,
Jumbled, unartificed, unformed, there lay
The earth, primeval waters and the skies.

Just so my mind, devoid of faculties,
Locked in my body's gross and heavy clay,
Unformed, unfinished, idled time away
When Love's bow pierced it through, shot from your eyes.

Love finished nature's half-done work in me,
Through Love my inner self found purity;
My life, my creative power – these gifts are Love's.

36

His flame gave my blood heat that will not cool,
And shaking me with beating wings, he moves
In sympathy with him my thoughts, my soul.

LIII

I saw – reflex hostility from you –
My hope fall to the earth, still green as grass;
It's not made out of rock, but brittle glass,
And my desires were broken clean in two.

Lady, where Heaven placed the love I know,
Who hold my whole life in your hand, you raise
Too fierce a war on one who gives you praise,
Depriving my heart of sweet pity too.

Well, if you like, erode my strength with pains –
For all that death strips out my nerves and veins,
I will be yours. And Chaos will invoke

Again its ancient misrule sooner than
A beauty, a love which is not your own
Could bend my captive back beneath its yoke.

LIV

That gentle way of speaking, honeyed words
That lie engraved deep in my memory;
That brow, Love's marble arch and majesty;
Sweet smiles; the savour that each kiss affords;

That golden hair; all those voluptuous curves;
Lilies and pinks, porphyry, ivory;
Those twin flames from which Heaven forces me
To drink deep gulps of venom that Love pours;

Those teeth, or rather clusters of white pearls;
Lips – inset rubies where the rose unfurls;
That voice that could allay a lion's rage,

Whose sweet song falls so poignant in my ear;
That perfect body, whose least beauties are
Each one enough to lay Troy under siege.

LV

Will I never see the season whose tides drag
Respite or peace, life or death to my door,
To draw the teeth of these cares that devour
A heart their rasping file has chafed to rags?

Will I never see my Naiad drawing back
The waves to point the harbour where I can moor?
Will I never come, like Ulysses, ashore,
Wearing her colours for my sail and flag?[1]

Will I never see those bright twin stars combine
Propitiously, and, like beacons, align
Their flames to guide my weary keel's last race?

Will I never see contending winds swing round
As one to run my ship gently aground,
Back again in the haven of her grace?

1 Classical mythology: Leucothea, a sea nymph (although the reference here
   is to a Naiad), gave Odysseus (Ulysses) her veil, which he wrapped around
   himself in order to reach land safely.

LVI

What malign destiny, what kind of star
Made me so mad so young, so full of pain?
What fate gave me cause always to complain
How I'm ruled by too harsh a master's law?

Which of the Sisters,[1] at my natal hour,
Blackened my life's thread to make sadness mine?
Which of the Demons[2] nursed me, made me drain
A breast full, not of milk, but bitter care?

Happy the dead whose bones lie in the ground!
Happier those in the night of Chaos found
Clasped to the black heart of its brutal mass!

Their rest is happy, out of feeling's reach.
I'm so tired. Must I feel too much, the wretch
Of love, a Sisyphus, a Tantalus?[3]

1 Classical mythology: the Sisters are the Fates; see note to XII.
2 For Demons, see note to XXXI.
3 For Sisyphus and Tantalus, see notes to XLIV.

LVII

Divine Du Bellay,[1] whose numerous rules
Your esoteric ardour made our law
Have re-equipped the boy Cytherea[2] bore
With bows and brands, arrows in quiverfuls,

If that sweet flame that seared your youth still rolls
On through you, sets your sacred breast on fire,
And if it still delights your ear to hear
Voices of lovers and their plaintive calls,

Listen to your Ronsard who sobs and mourns,
Pallid with fear, hung up in turmoil's storms,
His hands imploring vainly to the skies,

On a frail ship, no mast, no sail, no oar,
Far from the port where my Lady, like a star,
Once led me by the beacon of her eyes.

1   Joachim Du Bellay (1522–60) was a friend and associate of Ronsard, a great
    poet and important theorist, considered second only to Ronsard amongst
    the poets of La Brigade (La Pléiade). See Introduction.
2   Classical mythology: Cytherea is Venus/Aphrodite.

LVIII

When headlong the sun's golden chariot dives
To lie down with the Old Man of the Deep,[1]
And when the night slips its blindfold of sleep,
Drenched in oblivion, across our eyes;

Then Love, that gnaws away and undermines
The tottering ramparts of my reason's keep,
Flies post-haste like a warrior to shape
Arms for the fight from shades and dream-device.

It's then my reason and that cruel God
Rejoin their constant battle, head to head,
Their thousandfold duel that still escalates:

So matched, Love couldn't claim the victor's part
If not for my thoughts, that throw wide the gates,
My own troops are such traitors to my heart.

1   Classical mythology: the Old Man of the Sea is a figure usually identified
    with Proteus, father of Thetis (see note to XXXII). Proteus was a sea god who
    could change into an infinite number of forms.

LIX

Like a roebuck, when the spring dissolves away
The biting frost cold winter crystallised,
In search of honeyed leaves to graze on, flies
Out of his native woods at break of day;

Alone and safe, far from the hounds that bay
For blood, up mountain slopes, down valley sides,
By flowing waters deep seclusion hides,
He roams where chance leads, playful, wild and free;

His free spirit suspects no snare, no bow,
Until his life is taken at a blow,
One murderous arrow his last heartbeats bloody:

That's how I wandered, with no fear of hurt,
In my youth's April, that day her eye shot
A thousand arrows straight into my body.

LX

No sight of daybreak that ignites the rose,
No lilies thronging where the rivulet glides,
No lute's sound, and no birdsong ramified
Through woodland, no gold set with precious stones;

No open-throated Zephyr when it blows,
No vessel roaring as it stems the tide,
No nymph's dance by the gurgling water's side,
No universal flowering as spring grows;

No armed camp where the serried lances cross,
No green cave's entrance carpeted with moss,
No forest where the treetops crowd and cluster,

No sacred silence in the high crag's shadow –
None of these give such pleasure as one meadow[1]
Where hopelessly my hopes go out to pasture.

1   In this, as well as in the following sonnet and elsewhere in the cycle, there
    may be a play on the name of the estate owned by Cassandra Salviati's
    husband, Pray, and the word here translated as 'meadow', *pré*.

LXI

I saw a Naiad[1] walking in a field:
She wandered like a flower through the flowers,
Gathering their colours with that grace of hers,
Wearing a simple skirt, her hair unfurled.

She looked at me: my reason sickened, reeled;
My brow grew troubled, my eyes filled with tears,
My heart froze: such a mass of painful fears
That look stamped on my freedom in this world.

There I felt running through my eyes a sweet
New venom, subtly mixed to infiltrate
The soul where it feels sorrow's fiercest sting.

I've never sacrificed for my health's sake
Oxen or ewes, but I've flamed at the stake
On Love's fire, as my own burned offering.

1   Classical mythology: Naiads were water-nymphs.

LXII

When those beautiful eyes pronounce me dead
And banish me below before my day,
And when the Fate[1] has shown my steps the way
To the happier banks across the watershed;

Caves, meadows, forests – when my hour is fled,
Weep for my wrongs, and don't turn me away,
But grant me shade beneath your branches' sway,
A place of peace for my eternal bed.

And may some lovestruck poet come and take
Some pity here on my unhappy fate,
And carve this in one of the cypress trees:

'Here lies a lover whom the Vendôme bore,
And pain killed in this wood, for loving more
Than he should his Lady's beautiful eyes.'

1 For the Fate see note to XII.

LXIII

Whoever would see one still young ally
Beauty with purity of soul and pair
Sweet modesty with a majestic air,
All virtues with all amiability;

Whoever would look a goddess in the eye,
And see the one new sight for many a year,
Should view the beauty of this Lady here,
My mistress (or so goes the common cry),

And learn how Love can laugh at us and bite,
How he can cure, and how he kills for spite;
And then he'll say, 'Strange things are happening!

43

Earth borrowed Heaven's beauty; now earth even
Has taken beauty's self clean out of heaven,
If now earth holds so beautiful a thing.'

LXIV

The rainbow's shifting colours cannot span
So broad a spectrum on the bright sun's brow
When Juno brings her rainstorms driving through
And pours out waters to sustain the land;

Nor does Jupiter, arming his vengeful hand,
Redden the skies with such a lightning show,
Strafing Epirean[1] peaks with the thunder's blow,
Chastising pride where the Mausoleum stands;[2]

Nor does the sun shine forth such lovely beams
When morning comes to show his torch's flames
Shaking their golden hair, as when I saw

My Lady put on all her beauties, ignite
The fire in her eyes, step into the light,
That first day her charms filled my soul with awe.

1 Epirean: for Epirus, see note to VIII.
2 The Mausoleum was the legendary tomb of King Mausolos at Halicarnassus
   in Caria (modern Turkey).

LXV

When I catch sight of your fine burnished hair
That strips the Graces[1] of their fabled crown,
Your beautiful eyes that outshine the sun,
Your sweet blush no cosmetic fraud put there,

Head down, I weep and groan for what I bear,
Being the one (and yet grace should atone
For fault) who by his poetry's low tone
Betrays the glories that your beauties wear.

I know I should conduct my adoration
Of you in silence; yet the ulceration
Of love that burns my heart enchants my tongue.

And so, my All, if I've unworthily
Spent ink and voice to turn your grace to song,
It's destiny, not art, leads me astray.

1   For the Graces, see note to XV.

LXVI

Sky, open air, winds, plains, bare mountain slopes,
Vine-covered hills and forests growing green,
Serpentine rivers, rippling mountain streams,
Clearings in copses and you, green-leaved groves,

Half-open cave-mouths where the thick moss grows,
Fields, buds, flowers, grass pearled with the dewdrops' sheen,
Rolling dales, shores where golden beaches gleam,
And you, high crags, refuge my verses chose,

At our parting, pain and rage choked my goodbyes:
I couldn't say the word to those fine eyes
That, near, far, captivate me utterly;

And so I beg you, sky, air, winds, plains, mountains,
Copses and forests, riverbanks and fountains,
Caves, fields, flowers – say goodbye to her for me.

LXVII

Looking her in the eyes, my chosen girl,
I said to her: only you please my heart;
You nourish me with Love, so sweet a fruit
No other goodness satisfies my soul.

Love's archer, who takes good minds for his kill,
And doesn't condescend to waste his darts
Elsewhere, thicks my blood with cold fear, that starts
If I just see or speak to her at all.

No – there's no way that loving is a pain:
It's a noble sickness, whose bittersweet flame
– More sweet than bitter – burns us up inside.

I'd be twice, three times happy if Love would
Kill me, and with Tibullus[1] as my guide
I wandered there beneath the lovers' wood.

1 Tibullus (c. 55–19 BC) was a Roman elegiac love poet.

LXVIII

Those eyes, that could make savages refined,
Dissolving all pride in humility,
And with their subtle temper purify
The most earth-bound, dull spirits of the mind,

Their beauty's caught my love in such a bind
No other holds my heart beneath its sway,
And I think if one day I failed to see
Those fine eyes' light I'd lie caught in death's hand.

What the wide air is to the birds, the fresh
Woods are to stags, what waters are to fish,
Your beautiful eyes are to me. Light, full

Of a divine fire, that burns me with such passion,
In giving me my being and my motion,
Aren't you the Intelligence that moves my soul?

LXIX

When my girl was born to the world then straight
Behind came Honour, Virtue, Knowledge too,
Grace, Beauty, Chastity: debating who
Should have power in her to predominate.

First one would lay claim to that joyful state,
And then another want her close by, so
It might have turned into an endless row
Had Jupiter not silenced all debate.

'Now girls,' he said, 'It isn't right that one
Virtue should get to live in her alone:
So I want some accommodation here.'

The deal was struck; faster than he could decree,
Each occupied in perpetuity
Her lovely body in an equal share.

LXX

With what medicinal plant, what root the moon
Bewitched, what salve, what liquid panacea
Should I best soothe the wound in my heart here
Whose dire infection threads from bone to bone?

No magic charm of verse, no medicine, stone,
Extract or drug can make my symptoms clear;
I feel my strength bit by bit disappear,
Dragged off in Charon's ferry[1] all too soon.

Love, you who know which herbs have healing power
And who gave me this wounded heart, now cure
My sickness; show me what skills you can muster.

Near Troy you struck Apollo with your dart:[2]
I've felt the same sharp sting in my own heart;
Stop wounding both the pupil and the master.

1 Classical mythology: Charon is the ferryman who carries the shades of the
  dead across the river Styx to the underworld.
2 Classical mythology: for Apollo's love for Cassandra, see note to XXXVI and
  Introduction. See also note to XXXII on Apollo.

LXXI

Already Mars had fixed his choice on me
To trumpet in my verse the founder of France,
Francus; and used my rage to hone his lance
That stamped his hallmark on my poetry;[1]

Already Gaul echoed with havoc's cry
And iron sparkled in the Seine's bright dance,
And Francus brought Paris its inheritance,
The Trojan name and Asia's chivalry,

When that Boy Archer from whose back wings sprout,
Wounding me to the bone with one crack shot,
Ordained me priest to his high mysteries.

Farewell to arms. The myrtle Venus bears
Yields nothing to the laurel Apollo wears[2]
When Love with his own hand confers the prize.

1   The reference is to Ronsard's long-contemplated epic on the subject of the
     mythological origins of France, named *La Franciade* after its hero Francus,
     the name given there to Astyanax, son of Hector, who was the brother of
     Cassandra. Four books out of a projected twenty-four were published in
     1572. After the death of Charles IX, the poem's patron, the poem appears to
     have been abandoned. Mars as the god of war is a nominal patron of the
     poem.
2   Classical mythology: Venus as goddess of love is a patron of love poetry,
     and Apollo the god of poetry itself, and in particular, heroic poetry. Myrtle
     symbolises love poetry, laurel heroic poetry.

LXXII

Love, why when I write does the godlike grace
Not visit me, for all I have the will?
You'd be eclipsed by my poetic skill,
Orpheus, enchanter of old rocks in Thrace.[1]

Higher than Pindar, even Horace,[2] I'd trace
My flight, so I could make your godhead trail
A book of such profundity and scale
That Du Bellay[3] would offer up his place.

Not even Laura flies the universe,
With such life on the wings of Tuscan verse[4]
(Which our age has the taste to rate so high)

As your name, which gives French verse its élan,
Victorious over King and common man,
Would soar on the wings of my poetry.

1 Classical mythology: Orpheus is the mythological arch-poet and musician
  of Thrace at whose song rocks were moved to follow him.
2 Pindar and Horace are Greek and Latin poets respectively, the models
  Ronsard had taken for his Odes (1550).
3 For Du Bellay see note to LVII.
4 Laura is the Lady in the *Canzoniere* of Petrarch (the Tuscan).

LXXIII

Love lured me where my Circe, my enchantress,
Holds me imprisoned in her iron chains;
It wasn't taste of wine that poison stains,
Nor yet the juice of herbs black art enhances.

By the avenging sword of brave Odysseus,
And moly Mercury prescribed, the change
Began, no sooner than the draft was drained,
To overpower the powers of necromancers;[1]

So in the end Odysseus' flock could be
Restored to their first skin, man's dignity,
And sense, that had before senselessly slipped.

But to restore my brain to sanity
Would call a new Astolfo[2] here for me,
My reason's strayed so blindly in eclipse.

1 Classical mythology: the reference is to the episode in the *Odyssey* where
  members of Odysseus' crew are transformed into pigs by the potions of the
  enchantress Circe. Odysseus attacked with his sword after Hermes had
  given him moly, a herb, to make him immune to the potion.
2 In *Orlando Furioso* by Ariosto, Astolfo is the character who restores reason
  to Orlando.

LXXIV

It was the elements and stars that, thrown
Together, forged the rays of what I call
My sun, your eye, that has no parallel
In beauty, nowhere true comparison.

From those Iberian seas where the sun steeps down
To that in which its sleep grows soluble,
Love sees no comparable miracle
On which Heaven rains so many graces down.

That eye first taught me what power love imparts:
It came to make the first cut through my heart,
A target for the arrows that it fires.

It made my soul desire virtue it lacked,
To fly away on the unbeaten track
Up into the most beautiful ideas.

LXXV

I contrast, hold this crystal to your eyes:
This will reflect back my soul's murderer;
From this, bright flame goes flashing through the air,
Your eyes burn me in sacred sacrifice.

Fortunate mirror, as my symptoms arise
From seeing the beauty that sets me on fire
Too much, reflect my Lady too much there,
Like me, you'll waste with feelings just like these.

For all I'm jealous, you have my respect,
Reflecting fine eyes in which Love inspects
Himself, and where his bow's concealed within.

51

Go on then, mirror, but keep careful watch
Lest Love look straight back through her eyes to scorch
Your glass, and you get burned as I have been.

LXXVI

Not all the loving night's contending passions
Nor all the pleasures loves can comprehend,
Nor the kind interchanges lovers blend
Can equal one of my mortifications.

Hope, it's by grace of your great expectations
I can find rest from pains that cloud my mind;
Through you alone my fierce emotions find
Some sweet oblivion from their agitations.

So blessed be this sickness unto death
And that sweet yoke that takes away my breath;
Blessed be my anxiety of thought,

Blessed her sweetness in my memory,
And yet more blessed her eyes' thunderbolt
That sears my life in fire that freezes me.

LXXVII

Cursed be the bloodline of the Gorgon's face[1]
Which was the venomous snakes' primal source!
Helen, when trampling over them, you ought
Not to have broken backs, but destroyed the race.[2]

We spent the other day in a green space,
My girl and I, tying flowers in sweet knots;
Between us stood a jug of cream we'd brought,
With curd cheese clotted on its straw like ice.

A writhing snake with venom in its tooth
Shot – hidden evil – from the undergrowth
Across that foot to which I set my knee.

My heart froze, seeing that vile monster's raid,
And then I cried out, thinking it had made
Me a new Orpheus, her, Eurydice.[3]

1 Classical mythology: the Gorgon is Medusa, who had snakes for hair. See
   note to VIII.
2 Classical mythology: the reference to Helen relates to a story in Nicander's
   Theriaca in which Helen, returning from Troy, broke the back of a snake
   called the blood-letter.
3 Classical mythology: Eurydice, wife of Orpheus (see note to LXXII), died
   after being bitten by a snake.

LXXVIII

How happy, little spaniel, you would be
Had you the wit to know your happiness,
To stretch yourself out in her arms like this
And sleep held in her breast so lovingly!

While – look at me – I'm weakening wretchedly;
Too knowing, quick to grasp my destinies,
Seeking too much, alas, while young, to seize
The causes of things, I find misery.

I'd rather be some rustic villager,
Silly and senseless, no judgement to call
My own, or scrape work as a woodlander:

Then I'd have no feeling in love at all.
It's too much wit that hurts me: I despair
Because I'm over-analytical.

LXXIX

If, Lady, it's in your arms I meet death,
I would be glad; I couldn't wish to have
A greater honour in this world than to give
My soul flight, kissing you, pressed to your breast.

Let him whose bosom Mars' fires stir from rest
Go off to war, and let him rage and rave
At years and failing powers, glad to receive
Cold Spanish steel struck home into his chest.

I'm more the coward: all I ask's to crown
A hundred years' inglorious unrenown
By dying, spent, in your sweet lap, Cassandra.

For I'm mistaken, or it's happier
To die like that than have honour to spare
And live a short life, like an Alexander.

LXXX

To see at once the fields and waterside
My warrior girl inhabits with my heart,
Kind sun, tomorrow, rise early, depart,
Ascend your chariot, make haste and drive.

These are the fields where her beautiful eyes
Command me by the power of love they exert
To die, so sweetly, there's no better part
Of life than breathing such a sweet death's sighs!

See on the right, a little past the line
Of banks, her angel's face, alone there, shines,
My one jewel, that I covet and desire.

54

And there no spring exists, and no green place
But that reflects within itself the trace
Of her beautiful eyes, beautiful hair.

LXXXI

Forgive me, Plato,[1] if I can't agree
That under that arched vault, the gods' domain,
Whether beyond our world or on deep plains
The Styx[2] winds through, there's no vacuity.

If air fills out that liquid vault, tell me
Where can so many tears my eyes have drained,
Such sighs I've sobbed to the skies, be contained,
When Love gives free rein to my mourning cry?

Void space exists, or, if there is none there,
It wasn't filled by pressure of the air:
But rather Heaven, taking pity, lying

Open to take the weight my sorrow bears,
Is filled up from all sides, just by my tears,
And these verses I write as I lie dying.

1 Plato held that, in the words of the later cliché, 'nature abhors a vacuum'.
2 Classical mythology: the Styx is one of the rivers of the underworld.

LXXXII

I die, Paschal,[1] die every time I see
Her look so beautiful: her brow, mouth, eyes –
Those eyes, where Love takes home his victories
When he's shot a new arrow into me.

None of my blood, my veins, my marrow stay
Unchanged, and I seem snatched up to the skies
To sit amongst the gods, when fortune smiles
And brings her and me in proximity.

55

Why am I not a great king among men?
She'd take her place, my queen beside me, then.
But being nothing, I have to estrange

Myself and leave her beauty well alone:
I daren't approach, lest I feel one look change
My eyes to rivers and my heart to stone.

1 Pierre de Paschal (1522–65) was a friend of Ronsard, a Latin orator and histo-
riographer.

LXXXIII

If ever man was happy in his love
I am that happy man, I here confess,
Serving a mistress of such loveliness
Whose beautiful eyes don't cause me to grieve.

I desire only this desire I have.
Her honour, beauty, virtue, gentleness
Are like the flowers that grace her youthfulness,
Which I adore, like a pure saint above.

If anyone then would deny her grace
And beauty can erase all beauty's trace,
And I'm contented in my love at last,

I call him out in front of Love, I call
To prove to him, just as my heart stands fast,
So she is the most beautiful of all.

LXXXIV

Lady I love, it is to you I owe
My life, heart, body, my blood and my mind.
Looking in your eyes, Love himself defined
For me all good that since then I pursue.

My heart that burns in love's desire for you
Is held tight by your grace, so strong a bind
One look from your eyes makes it comprehend
All honour, love and courtesy can do.

The man is made of lead, or has no eyes,
Who, seeing you, can't see all Heaven lies
There, in your beauty that's unparalleled.

Your good grace has power to attract a rock,
And when no day breaks and the world turns dark
Your beautiful eyes would light up the world.

LXXXV

Beauty, who hold my heart with gentleness,
And who have kept throughout this whole past year
My soul in your eyes as a prisoner,
Making its life such lovely languidness;

O why can't I reach high into the skies
To heaven, that dictates our fate's career?
I'd change its course, give it new paths to steer,
And turn my sadness into happiness.

I'm just a man though, and a man must grin
And bear cruel Heaven's violent discipline,
Which orders me to die for your eyes' sake.

So, Lady, I come giving, as bells toll
The New Year, gifts Heaven orders me to make:
My heart, mind, body, my blood and my soul.

LXXXVI

Water and fire are the two powers that drive
This system: I can feel them fill me through;
Divine powers, who divinely hoisted to
My back this divine burden I must heave.

All things terrestrial or divine, in brief,
Derive their origin from just these two.
Both live on equal terms in me; I too
Live in them: they are all I can conceive.

And nothing other than them comes from me,
The two born out of me alternately:
When my eyes, having wept too much, abate,

Then, raised by hope that comes to soothe my pain,
A furnace of flame breathes out from my heart
And suddenly my tears begin again.

LXXXVII

If the poet through whose verse Greek armies throng[1]
Had seen your eyes that hold me in their thrall,
He'd not have started on Mars' feats at all
And great Achilles would have died unsung.

Had Paris, who saw Cyprus' goddess[2] among
The mountain valleys, and felt passion's thrill,
Seen you fourth, he'd have made his judgement fall
On you, and Venus, unprized, move along.

But should it happen, by the will of the skies
Or by the bolt shot from your lovely eyes,
I sing your triumph in exalted verse,

And, a new Cygnus,[3] I am heard to cry,
No myrtle and no laurel then will be
Worthy of you or worthy of my brows.[4]

1   The Greek poet is Homer, hence the references to Achilles and the
    Judgement of Paris.
2   Classical mythology: Cyprus' goddess is Venus/Aphrodite.
3   Classical mythology: the reference to Cygnus probably relates to the King
    of Liguria in Ovid, who mourned his friend Phaeton's death by the river
    Eridanos and was turned by the gods into a swan. The myth was also refer-
    enced by Petrarch. 'Cygne', as well as being the French equivalent of the
    Latin name Cygnus, also means 'swan', and there could be a parallel refer-
    ence to the myth of Orpheus (see note to LXXII),who was transformed after
    his death into the constellation called the Swan.
4   For the meaning of laurel and myrtle, see note to LXXI.

LXXXVIII

To sing how fortune, stripped out from the stars,
Flows into her who wears my strength away,
And praise her mind that gives exclusively
The peak of rarest virtues its regards,

And sing those looks, love's sharpened points she scores
With her fine eyes deep in the heart of me,
I'd need, not my own ardent poetry,
But Rapture, that stung Pontus[1] into verse.

I'd need a lyre – Du Bellay's from Anjou,[2]
A Dorat,[3] Siren[4] of Limousin, too,
And a Belleau,[5] who, living, was my friend:

Our habits, studies, youth were all allied;
But now he swells the pale throng of the dead:
He went before me to his evening's end.

1 Pontus is Pontus de Tyard (1521–1605) a poet and friend of Ronsard who
   formed part of La Brigade (La Pléiade).
2 For Du Bellay, see note to LVII.
3 Dorat is Jean Dorat (1508–88), a poet and friend of Ronsard who formed part
   of La Brigade (La Pléiade).
4 The Sirens (see note to XVI) were legendary for the sweetness of their voices.
5 For Belleau, see note to XXIII. He died in 1577: this sonnet was amended in
   later editions to incorporate this tribute.

LXXXIX

To be poor and give all you have away,
To feign a smile and have your heart in tears,
To hate what's true and love what just appears,
Possess all and have nothing to enjoy;

To be free and drag shackles all the way,
To be brave and beset with coward fears,
To want to die and live, as fate decrees,
And to invest your all, profitlessly;

To bear forever, as your servile brand,
Shame on your brow and dead loss in your hand,
To weave incessantly, from thoughts that spring

Out of high courage, new thread for your loom:
These are the things that make my soul a home
To dubious hope and certain suffering.

XC

Eye, who command my eyes on your own terms,
Like a sun, god of what light comes to me;
Smile, who, constraining my sweet liberty,
Metamorphose me through a hundred forms;

You, silver tear, who fall into my flames
When you pretend to see my misery;
Hand, who hold my heart in captivity,
That prisoner a chain of roses tames;

I so belong to you, and feeling so
Dyed my blood with the flawlessness of you,
That neither time nor death, for all their power,

Can stop me always carrying around
Graven in my soul, at my heart's deep core,
An eye and a smile, a tear and a hand.

XCI

If only images of things that meet
Our eyes persuade our eyes that things can be,
And if my eye hasn't the power to see
Unless some object stands in front of it,

Why didn't the whole world's creator fit
Me bigger eyes, better equipping me
With grand scope to frame the grand illusion she
Projects around my life, imprisoning it?

Certainly Heaven, too churlish to share
Her it alone made, where it alone saw
Beauty raised to idea of the divine,

Jealously guarding such a precious prize,
Hoodwinked the whole world and blinded my eyes,
So she alone was seen by it alone.

XCII

Within the crystal of a stream the light
Silvered, in April, a pearl caught my eye,
Whose luminescence so enraptured me
My mind's impervious to other thought.

Its roundness glistened, a pure, simple white,
Outshining all in luminosity:
I could admire that pearl untiringly,
Destiny marks it so for my pursuit.

Bending a hundred times to fish the depths,
My heart on fire, I reached my arm and dipped,
And I might hold that pearl now, feel that pleasure,

Had not an Archer, envious of my prize,
Troubled the water and dazzled my eyes,
To hold alone the rights to such a treasure.

XCIII

Lady, the first day of the month of May
I felt your beautiful eyes in my heart:
Brown, sweet, kind, full of laughter and delight,
That could strike fire from ice – incendiary.

Memory fires me with their breaking day:
I fall in love with them just at the thought.
O my heart's blessed murderers! I start,
Feeling your power deep in the soul of me.

Eyes, where the key to all my thought's held fast,
Rulers of me, who have the power to blast
With one look these wits feeling has worn through,

Your beauty wounds my heart, so palpable
A force, I should enjoy the sight of you
For longer, or just not see you at all.

XCIV

If her golden hair curls down lazily
Or strays in two unrolling waves around
Her breast, swayed here and there, bright vagabonds
That purl around her neck coquettishly;

Or if some richly ornamented tie
Which many rubies and pearls cluster round
Clasps these two tresses in one flood of blonde,
Happiness flows right to the heart of me.

What pleasure – no – what marvel then appears
Whenever her hair, tucked behind her ears
Lends her the look a Venus might display?

Or when she wears a cap to play Adonis,[1]
And you can't tell if she's a girl or a boy,
Her beauty lurks in such ambiguous promise?

1 Classical mythology: Adonis was a youth of legendary beauty loved by
Venus/Aphrodite.

XCV

Dew-drenched Aurora,[1] scattering her hair's
Dishevelment, filled up the Indian sky,
And now Heaven reddened with long streaks of dye,
The various enamels morning wears,

When she saw that girl whom my heart adores
Bind up her hair: its golden light flashed by,
Outshining hers and blinding every eye
To her and to all Heaven in its course.

And then Aurora tore her hair, disgraced
As she was, and, in tears, she hid her face,
Mere mortal beauty had caused her such pain.

And then she heaved so many sighings forth
That from her sighs a wind was brought to birth,
A fire from her shame, from her eyes, a rain.

1   Classical mythology: Aurora is the goddess of dawn.

XCVI

Take this rose, that is loveable like you,
Who are the rose of all the loveliest roses,
Flower of the freshest flowers spring uncloses,
Whose scent ravishes me from all I know.

Take this rose, take to your breast what comes too –
My heart that no light pair of wings defaces:
It stands fast: cruel wounds in a hundred places
Couldn't prevent its faith from staying true.

One difference separates the rose from me:
A single sun sees this rose born and die,
A thousand suns have looked on my love's birth,

This process that acts never-endingly.
I would to God such love-captivity
Had lasted, like a flower, one day on earth.

XCVII

After my tears, you should have tears to shed,
Sad house, for this grim absence that remains
Now that fine eye is gone which, present, reigned
As your sun: no – it was my sun instead.

For such wrongs, Love, so many times I've bled,
How a long visit makes good all my pain!
When, shamed, at any time I think again
How in one moment I lost all I had,

Well, I say then, farewell, disdainful beauty!
A wood, rock, stream, a mountain will do duty
To drive you far away, out of my eyes,

But not out of my heart, so it won't go
In hot pursuit of you, and live in you
Not me, because that's where its true love lies.

XCVIII

Everything hurts, but nothing grieves me more
Than to be exiled from my Lady's eyes,
Which took away in their bright rays the keys
To sweetest pleasures my soul knew before.

Out of my head torrents of water pour,
And now I faint away, choked up with sighs,
Losing the fire whose sacred flames were guides,
The sole lights leading my thought's ship to shore.

Since that day I first felt its searing heat,
I've seen no other beauty to compete,
Nor will I. But if only I could see,

Just before dying, that wild creature, just
With one glance, vow a shred of hope to me
In Love's assault, where all my hope has ceased.

XCIX

Now, jealous Sun, envying Love his pride,
Sun masquerading with a pallid face,
Who three days has confined my girl to base,
Alone indoors, while rain pours down outside;

Now I don't think so many lovers tried
Your heart: they're just old poets' fantasies.
Had Love touched your imagination, crazed
It with this pain, you'd show a caring side.

With your rays sharpened into horns you would,
In kindness to me, have struck through the cloud,
Turning the stormy weather calm and even.

So go and hide, you rustic old cow-master:
You don't deserve to shine, a torch in heaven;
You just lead oxen, herder, out to pasture.[1]

1 Classical mythology: a reference to the oxen herded by the Sun.

C

Whenever I see you, or when I think
Of you, a shiver flutters through my heart,
My blood thrills, and from one thought's fertile start
Another grows, so sweet's the theme they bring.

I feel all my nerves, my knees shuddering;
I'm wasting, drop by drop, like wax flames heat;
My reason falls down, powers I can't exert
Leave me cold, breathless, my pulse vanishing.

I'm like a dead man lowered to the grave,
So drawn, so grim is this pale face I have,
As I watch death strip consciousness away.

Still I delight in this pyre nonetheless.
So the same evil pleases both of us:
I'm pleased to die, and you're pleased to kill me.

CI

Dull in my body, duller in my wits,
I dragged myself around, a dumb, dead weight,
And, unaware what high rewards await
The Muse's servants, scorned her offices.

But from that day my love for you first hit,
It was to virtue that your eyes conveyed
And snatched me up; that's how I was remade,
The ignoramus turned sophisticate.

And so, my All, if I do anything,
Make fitting songs about your eyes to sing,
It's you cause such effects in me, just you.

It's from you I take all my finished grace;
It's you inspire me, you in me create,
If I do good things, all the good I do.

CII

In my soul's eye I see continually
That beauty that lives in my heart and stays;
No mountain, wood nor river ever frees
Me from her power by thought to speak to me.

Lady, who know my faith and constancy,
Please look and see how time that vanishes
Through seven years took not the smallest piece
Of that sweet pain I bear for you away.

I never tire of having that to bear,
Nor would I, were I wearied out down here,
Reborn a thousand times in a thousand forms.

But I'm already weary of my heart:
It grieves me: we can't be on such good terms
As once we were, since you hounded it out.

CIII

I scatter seedcorn on the barren sands,
I sound to the abysmal depths in vain,
Unasked, at all hours, here I come again,
And I let my youth fritter through my hands.

My vow's nailed my life where her portrait hangs;
My heart's turned into sulphur by her flame;
For her eyes I bear, with no hope of gain,
Ten thousand wrongs – yet not one grievance stands.

Someone who understood my life's true state
Would never want to choose a lover's fate.
I can feel myself burning hot and cold.

My pleasures are all steeped in bitterness;
I live on worry, waste with mournfulness –
This is what loving too much has entailed.

CIV

One image haunts my eyes both night and day –
The sacred portrait of her angel's face:
Whether I'm writing, or I interlace
My verse in lute strings, it comes constantly.

For God's sake, see how this beautiful eye
Imprisons me, and how there's no release;
How it snares my heart in complexities
Thought ravels up to make a hell for me.

Oh, the great evil, when our soul is taken
Captive by monsters fantasy awakens!
Judgement sleeps on still in its prison cell.

Deceiver Love, why would you want to make
Me think that whiteness is a form of black,
The sensual outranks the rational?

CV

As you go by, I don't start from the blocks
To soil you with some love that honour scorns;
So stay a while: Locrian Ajax warns
Me not to force you, from Gyraean rocks.[1]

There Neptune, hearing blasphemy that mocked
The gods, smashed in that head shame could not turn
With one huge rock, amid the raging storm;
'Evil men meet death when they run amok.'

He wanted – evil – to rape you himself,
When fear made you embrace, imploring help,
The feet of the avenging Greek Minerva;

I just want at your altar to give this,
My pure heart, if it please you to permit
That by its immolation it might serve you.

1 Classical mythology: at the sack of Troy Cassandra took refuge in the
Temple of Athena/Minerva. Ajax (the 'Lesser' Ajax, from Locris) raped her
and was punished by Neptune/Poseidon, who crushed him on a rock at sea
called Gyraea.

CVI

My Lady, I'm a thief for loving you;
If I want to live, I must go and steal
The looks from your beautiful eyes, and spoil
By my look your look that can lay me low.

I starve just for your beautiful eyes, so
Double the power they have to overfill
My heart with joy, and double my days, all
My life being just a spark their flames once threw.

A single look you're pleased to leave behind
Feeds me three days; then I come back to find
(Once I've exhausted that first piece of food)

And steal my living from adversity,
Driven to thieving that forbidden fruit,
Not out of pleasure, but necessity.

CVII

Gripped by the name that freezes me in fire,
Keeping my sweet Grace[1] in my memory,
I plant here one plant chosen carefully,
Next to whose greenness emeralds disappear.

Every adornment a great king might wear –
Beauty, grace, knowledge, honour, ability –
Are rooted in this Marguerite you see
Which all through Heaven and Earth perfumes the air.

Divine flower where all my hopes now remain,
May manna endlessly fall, fall again
On that face each new weather front renews.

And may you never shrink from the approach
Of girl, or honey-bee, or sickle's touch,
Or of the frisking lamb with his sharp hooves.

1 For the Graces, see note to XV.

CVIII

Since that day when the random arrow scored
The rock-face of my memory with your name,
When your look, from which all your glory flamed,
Made palpable what lightning your eyes flared,

This heart a stinging thunderbolt had seared,
Avoiding the new victory you'd claimed,
Hid under your ivory curves and aimed
For shelter underneath your loving head.

And mocking my wound's bitterness in there,
It plays amid the safety of your hair,
Delighting in the fires you set ablaze;

And it so loves its hostess that it will
Never return: it leaves me pale and chill,
Just like a spirit fleeing from its grave.

CIX

My sickness is grave: all cures fall so short
For pain whose bitterness nothing can soothe,
From down beneath my feet to up above
The top of my head, there's no healthy part.

The eye that held the key to all my thought,
Rather than be my shining star and move
To guide me through the tides of violent love,
Has wrecked my ship against a reef of spite.

Awake, in dreams, murderous anxiety,
Fierce tiger, sinks a thousand teeth in me,
Grasping my heart, my lungs, my entrails fast.

And that intrusive thought, that crowds me so,
Like a fierce vulture, never lets me go –
A new Prometheus,[1] at my lifeblood's cost.

1   For Prometheus, see note to XII.

CX

Love, if my fever were to rise and gain,
If your bow wounds me with another shot,
I fear I'd drop before my days were out
The still green burden of this human skin.

I feel my heart's strength starting to decline,
Transforming it, to bring death closer yet,
Before the blazing of my ardent thought
Not to green wood, but a powder magazine.

For me that was the day ill fortune frowned
Then, when I gulped love's witch's brew straight down,
That drink one look poured me in such long measures.

O, I'd have known good fortune if Love had
That very day, to help me, left me dead,
And not kept me sick so long at his pleasure.

CXI

So gently my heart's probed, remembering
That honey-sweetened, gall-embittered season
When I lost both my senses and my reason,
No other pleasure pacifies the sting.

No way do I want this wound bandaging,
This wound Love made, for healing powers to seize on;
No way do I want to be sprung from prison,
To let my hopes find some new place to spring.

73

More than I flee death I flee liberty,
For fear that I might see myself cut free
From that sweet fetter that so sweetly wounds,

And it's an honour seeing myself made
A martyr, in hope one day I'll be paid
A single kiss, for all my recompense.

CXII

Fortunate was the day, year, month and place,
The time of day when your eyes struck me dead,
Or if not dead, then at least petrified,
Medusa,[1] into a cold block of ice.

It's true the outward features of my face
Remain with me still, but my spirit, freed
To live in you, forgot the corpse it fled,
Leaving me here, bereft, a cold, dead mass.

Sometimes when, briefly, you let your eyes turn
On me, I feel a small fire start to burn
That reinvigorates me, warms my veins,

And makes some little inroad on the cold.
But your looks only elongate my pains,
So irreversibly that first look killed.

1   For Medusa, see note to VIII.

CXIII

The archer Love lets all his arrows go
In one shot at me, yet no comfort's there,
Not one look, from the girl for whom I wear
My heart in my eyes, my thoughts on my brow.

A sun sheds ice that casts me solid now,
And I'm amazed my chill has not died here
In rays cast by an eye whose gentle fire
Burns in my heart to sear deep ulcers through.

I see my life's force weaken so in me
The feeblest stir my weak heart's jealousy,
So suffering grows, and heart diminishes.

And yet the pain that troubles my soul most
– Cruelty! – is that Love and Lady both
Know what I suffer, and could not care less.

CXIV

I saw my girl amongst a hundred ladies,
A crescent moon moving through lesser lights,
And with her eyes, lovelier than stars at night,
She put into the shade their loveliest beauties.

Within her breast there the immortal Graces,[1]
The twin Loves[2] and the Spirit of Delight
Went flitting round, like small birds that alight
Amongst the newest branches' fresh green spaces.

The ravished sky, seeing her so beautiful,
Rained roses down, lilies and garlands, all
Around her, in the middle of that place;

As if, in spite of winter's bitter cold,
By that love-stirring power her eyes hold,
Beautiful spring caught life's spark from her face.

1   For the Graces, see note to XV.
2   For the Loves, see note to XL. References to twins refer to the legend of Eros
    and Anteros, in which Anteros was given to Eros as a playmate when he
    was lonely, as a figure of love's inability to thrive without response.

CXV

Above all kings, their sceptres, wealth and fame,
I love this brow on which my Tyrant plays,
And that vermilion this fine cheek displays,
Which puts the Tyrian purple quite to shame.

All beauties in my eyes disgrace the name
Next to this breast, whose sighs heave to displace
Her bodice, under which there softly sways
A slight flux and reflux Venus might claim.

In the same way that Jupiter is calmed
When a Muse soothes him with her song's sweet balm,
So when I hear her singing I'm enraptured,

When intricate lute fingerings are joined
To her sweet voice in the 'Brawle of Burgoyne',[1]
Which she sang on the day that I was captured.

1   A brawle is a kind of dance form used in the music of Ronsard's time.

CXVI

That beauty to which my eyes are in thrall,
Who makes me live amid a thousand deaths,
Leashed up my hounds and followed in my steps,
Like Adonis and the golden Cyprian girl.[1]

And then a bramble[2] that hopelessly fell
In love like me with her arms' rosiness
Set flowing down them with its rough caress
A crimson liquid like a cordial.

The earth, then, that absorbed so carefully
That sacred blood, bore in its fertile way
The blood-red little flower such blood begets.

Just as from Helen once arose the flower
That took its beautiful surname from her,[3]
So from Cassandra they're called Cassandrettes.[4]

1 Classical mythology: for Adonis see note to XCIV. When Adonis was
   pricked by a rose thorn his blood turned white roses red. The Cyprian girl
   is Venus/Aphrodite.
2 Possibly another reference to the 'ronce (qui) ard' device connected with
   Ronsard's name: see note to XVI.
3 Classical mythology: elecampane or inula is a flower to which Helen of Troy
   gave her name, as it sprang where her tears fell.
4 The 'Cassandrette' is a campanula.

CXVII

At twenty, inoffensive, pure in thought,
Led by some blind, winged kid where fools rush in,
A young blood, with a mere lad's beardless chin,
Merry, robust, I came to pay you court.

But o, cruel lady, outraged by your spite,
I come back out inside an old man's skin,
My hair turned grey and all my good looks gone:
That's how the games, the tricks Love plays fall out.

Alas, what am I saying? Where would I go?
No other diet could satisfy me so.
You turn me, Love, to something like a quail,

That fattens taking poison for its food.
I don't want to eat any other meal
Or live elsewhere, your poison tastes so good.

CXVIII

I couldn't have lived without sighing here
Since that day when my Lady's eyes, where all
The Loves had gathered, poured into my soul
Sweet venom, filling my heart to the core.

My dear snow, and my dear and gentle fire,
See how I freeze and then how my flames roll:
Like wax flame's radiation melts to fuel,
I am consumed – and how little you care.

It's certain that my life is fortunate
To pour itself in joy and sorrow out
Under your eye, that wounds me day and night.

But still your beauty never reckons how
Affections poise affections to fall true,
How one Love with no brother gains no weight.[1]

1 For Loves see note to XL, and for the myth of Eros and Anteros see note to
   CXIV.

CXIX

You minister of Love and steadfastness,
Who can stir the profound depths of the soul,
And who blind eyes with your delusional
Perception, veil hearts in unknowingness,

Just go away, look for some new address,
Go somewhere else, deceive some other fool,
I don't want you to come back here at all,
Ill-starred and damned as you are, Hopefulness.

When Jupiter, that tyrant drunk with crime,
In his own father's blood incarnadined
His hands, taking gold from this earthly place,[1]

He left you, a new monster, forced to lie
Alone, deep in the vessel carried by
Pandora,[2] to delude the human race.

1 Classical mythology: Jupiter/Zeus, waging war on his father Saturn/
Chronos, brought an end to the Golden Age.
2 For Pandora see note to V.

CXX

Set free from reason and enslaved to passion,
Hunting an untamed creature now I chase
Up mountains, down banks where the rivers race,
Now through thickets of youth and misdirection.

I have my leash, misfortune's long connection,
I have my bloodhound, courage to excess,
My dogs, my ardour and my youthfulness,
And, for my huntsmen, I've hope and affliction.

But they, seeing how the more she's chased, the more
She stretches out the race and flees before,
Leaving their quarry, turn back onto me,

Daring to make my very flesh their food.[1]
It's pitiful (as to my shame I see)
When servants rule their masters' servitude.

1 Classical mythology: Actaeon, a hunter, saw Artemis/Diana bathing and in
punishment was transformed into a stag and then ripped apart by his own
hounds.

CXXI

Lady, Heaven doesn't want me to possess
The sweet reward my duty might deserve,
So I don't want it: I'm not pleased to have
Anything but wrongs for my services.

Since you're pleased that you cause my weaknesses,
I'm happy, and I can't hope to receive
A greater honour than that as I serve
I give your eyes my heart in sacrifice.

So if, despite myself, sometimes my hand
Transgresses, oversteps chaste love's commands,
Searching for what inflames me in your breast,

Chastise it with the lightning your eyes scatter
And burn it: living with no hands is better
Than my hand causing you to be displeased.

CXXII

Though six years have already flowed away
Since that day when Love with a wounding shot
Engraved the portrait deep within my heart
Of my meek-proud and proud-meek adversary,

I'm still glad that the light has shone on me
These late years, while that portrait lived and caught
Her beauty, that captured my mind and brought
A beautiful trajectory from the sky.

The single April of her springtime's prime
Makes gold, pearl and brocade adorn our time,
To which my Beauty's virtues were obscure,

As was the splendour that shone from her eyes.
I alone saw it: and I die for her:
No greater joy was given me by the skies.

CXXIII

If that great prince, inventor of the lyre,[1]
Who rises, waking, from his Indian bounds
And with an eye confused by sleep looks round,
Reviewing all things, here, there, everywhere,

Grieves still for that prize to which I aspire,
Am I not happy that same shot that once
Cut through the sun from edge to edge now wounds
My heart to cause the martyrdom we share?

Indeed, pain's soothed with pleasure in my heart,
To have dared to choose for my counterpart
So great a god: so in the countryside

The ox bent down beneath the yoke's dead weight
Can feel the burden grow more sweet and light
When he toils with another alongside.

1 Classical mythology: the prince is Apollo, god of the sun and of music and
poetry, a lover rejected by Cassandra. See note to XXXII, and Introduction.

CXXIV

That little dog, my Lady's acolyte,
Yapping, not recognising anyone;
That bird whose plaintive cries re-echo on,
A plangent sound all through the April night;

The gate where when the warmth gives way to heat
Milady communes with her thoughts alone;
That garden where her thumbnail reaps like corn
All of the flowers the Zephyr brings to light;

That dance in which the cruel arrow flew
Right through me, the new season come to renew
My sorrows, as in all the other years;

The look, the sacred word she speaks, her grace
I've pictured here in my heart's inmost place:
Bathe my eyes in two rivulets of tears.

CXXV

Hot-blooded Ruggiero, whom Love's fire misled,
Decoyed by that shape-shifting sorcery's lure,
So your new passion might be cooled once more,
You came and settled on Alcina's bed.[1]

Quenching your fire the one thought in your head,
Soaring above and weltering under her,
In such a lovely lady's arms, you there
Took what revenge on Love and her you could.

In a short time the gracious Zephyr's wind,
Luckily driving your ship from behind,
Drove it into its loving haven, home.

But when my ship is set to come ashore
A foul storm always blows up, drives it far
Further off, out to sea: such is my doom.

1 Ruggiero and Alcina are characters in Ariosto's *Orlando Furioso*. Ruggiero is
held captive by the enchantress Alcina on her magical island, and, forget-
ting his love for Bradamante, devotes himself to Alcina until rescued by the
sorceress Melissa.

CXXVI

I hate you, people: as witness I call
The Loir, Gâtine wood, the banks of the Braie,
Neuffaune wood and green willow groves that lie
Down in the corner next to Sabut hill.[1]

When I'm alone there, wandering at will
Far off, Love holds talks with me there to try
Not curing, but deepening my injury,
Out in these wilds that make my anguish hell.

There, Lady, step by step, my mind retraces
Your face, your mouth and then your fine eyes' graces,
Those archers that shoot too true to their marks;

Then making out your lovely counterfeit
In light on water, I sob one cry out,
And force groans from the hardest of the rocks.

1 The places named in the first four lines are all places near Ronsard's home
near Vendôme. For the Loir, see note to XVI.

CXXVII

It's not the heat that bakes earth's smouldering plains
On summer days that parch cracks in her face;
It isn't Procyon,[1] who dries to the lees
The tepid waters he, thirst raging, drains;

It's not that torch that sets the world in flames
With sparkling radiance that slowly dies;
In short, it isn't summer or its fires
That makes this furnace heat that sears my veins.

Your chaste fires, spirits of your lovely eyes,
Your sweet lightnings that re-ignite the skies –
These make my furnace flame perpetual;

And whether Phoebus[2] yokes his team to pass
Through Cancer or through Sagittarius,[3]
It's your eye that makes summer in my soul.

1   Procyon is a star in Canis Minor that precedes the Dog Star in the sky, hence
    heralding the 'Dog Days', the hottest time of the year between (approxi-
    mately) 24th July and 24th August.
2   Classical mythology: Phoebus is Apollo, here in his guise as the sun god. See
    note to XXXII.
3   The sun enters Cancer around 20th June and Sagittarius around 20th
    November.

CXXVIII

Neither this coral in whose double tier
These many pearls are set, jewels from the East,
Nor those fine lilies which Love on his knees
Dares kiss, and of which he can never tire;

Nor this fine gold that coiled in tangled wire
Playfully curls a thousand filigrees,
Nor these pinks that ideally harmonise
The white the lilies her face brings forth wear;

Nor the fine sunlit heaven of this brow,
Nor these twin eyebrows in their double bow
Passed the death sentence on this life of mine.

Just these fine eyes where the sure Archer came
To hide the fatal dart that bore my name
Finished my day before its evening time.

CXXIX

Say yes or no: without my self-deceit
Over how little love you seem to bear,
I couldn't, seeing my pain's so severe,
Lament so, write at such Petrarchan heat.

So if you want it, why refuse this sweet
Last gift, the hope of which consoles my care?
If not, why feed me hope dead as despair
So your seduction of me is complete?

One of your eyes hurls me deep down to hell,
The other, gentler, struggles just as well
To put me back in paradise again.

And so your eyes, to cause rebirth in me,
And then my death, turn me incessantly
Now into Pollux, now Castor his twin.[1]

1 For Castor and Pollux see note to XLIX.

CXXX

In the year fifteen hundred and forty-six
In her hair, a lady marred by cruelty
(As cruel as she was beautiful to me)
Bound up my heart which that hair had transfixed.

I thought then, like an inexperienced hick,
One born to suffer pain eternally,
Those massed curls might use their blonde witchery
Two or three days, no more, to hold me fixed.

That year passed by, and now begins one more:
I see myself, more even than before,
Caught in their snares, and when death sometimes would

Unravel this knot my pain twists to rope,
Love always, so his grip grows yet more hard,
Flatters my heart with unavailing hope.

CXXXI

Each year I order you a sacrifice,
My faithful place, where, trembling and afraid,
I first discovered this long, wasting trade
I have borne, Lady, doing your offices.

There is no better, surer, luckier place
For love's tormenting pain to be proclaimed
In Cyprus, or the happiest orchard shade
That Knidos, Amanthos or Eryx has.[1]

Had I the gold of some ambitious prince,
Place, you'd be a shrine of magnificence,
Ornate with gold, expense in everything,

86

Where lovers, by vows made in solemn prayer,
Jousting and fighting round your altar there,
Would immolate themselves as offerings.

1   Classical mythology: Cyprus, Knidos, Amanthos and Eryx are all places in
    the Ancient World associated with the cult of Venus/Aphrodite.

CXXXII

Glory of May, the last remains of spring,
Bouquet picked by the hand that makes me hers,
Whose beauties put to shame the little flowers
And make April a yearlong flourishing;

I sense, not in my nose but heart, your sting,
And in the wits that your scent overpowers;
It rises, vein to vein, up with such force
I sense your scent pervading everything.

So, come on, kiss me while our girl's away,
Please take my sighs, and take my tears from me:
They'll bring your colours to new life and light.

That way your flower will never fade and die:
Tears lend moist humour, sighs impassioned heat
For you to take root in my life one day.

CXXXIII

If they tell you Argus[1] is mythical,
Don't you believe it, good Posterity;
That's not a tale, it's pure reality:
To my cost I feel the truth of it all.

An Argus two eyes make formidable,
In human form – no dream, no fallacy –
Spies, watches, guards the beauty by which I
Am riven with doubt and made miserable.

If Argus didn't keep her in his sight
She'd still hang round my neck her pretty weight:
I know her nature's gentleness itself.

True Argus, you fill me with groans so deep,
Would a new Mercury might come to help –
Not to kill you, but just put you to sleep.

1   Classical mythology: Argus was a guard with countless eyes set by Juno/
Hera to guard the nymph Io, and who was killed by Mercury/Hermes.

CXXXIV

I liken your young beauty, and the way
It lives on in its springtime, always new,
To April, which makes flowers spring anew
In all its gladdest, greenest novelty.

Before you, cruelty will flee far away,
The cruellest season flees from April too;
It, like your face, is lovely through and through;
Its course is fixed, fixed like your loyalty.

It paints the banks, the forests and the plains,
You paint my verses with a riot of flowers;
It waters the farm labourers' toils and pains,

You wash my sorrows in vain hopefulness;
It makes the Heavens' tears fall to the grass,
You power two fountains from my eyes like rains.

CXXXV

Sweet beauty, who are my life's murderess,
You have a flint where your heart ought to be;
You make the life in me grow weak, and dry
Away in my love's passion to possess.

Young blood, that urges you to hear love's voice,
Couldn't part you from your frigidity;
Untamed and proud, your dearest hope's to stay
Inert, cold, served by no one, passionless.

Learn how to live, proud though you are to be cruel.
Don't save your beauty up for Pluto's hall:[1]
Take some small joy in loving, as you must.

We have to use life's sweetness to cheat death:
Then, feeling nothing, down beneath the earth,
The body's nothing any more but dust.

1   Classical mythology: Pluto's hall is the underworld, of which Pluto is the god.

Stanzas

When we're there in church we'll be
Kneeling down, and then we'll play
Pious pilgrims, in the guise
Of those folk who, praising God,
Humbly bend in prayer and nod
In the church's holiest place.

But when we're in bed we'll be
Intertwined, and then we'll play
Sensual creatures, in the guise
Of free lovers who resort
To the bedsheets, and in sport
Play a hundred pretty ways.

Why then, when I want to tear
With my teeth your lovely hair,
Kiss your mouth from which Love calls,
Touch this breast I gaze upon,
Do you play the little nun,
Locked within a cloister's walls?

Who do you keep your eyes for,
And your breasts that I adore,
And that brow, that pair of lips?
Is it Pluto's kiss you choose
Down in Hell, when Charon rows
You away there in his skiff?[1]

After your last exit here
Your frail shade below will bear
Just a little pallid mouth;
When I come to see you dead,
I won't tell the Shades how you'd
Been my lover in our youth.

You'll have no skin on your skull:
And your face, so beautiful,
Neither vein nor artery.
All you'll have are teeth like those
That grin out at you in rows
From heads in the cemetery.

So then, while life is so fine,
Change, my Lady, change your mind,
Don't deny your mouth to me.
You'll die all too quickly yet;
When that day comes, you'll regret
Treating me disdainfully.

Ah! I'm dying! Kiss me now!
Lady, ah, come closer to!
You flee like a trembling fawn.
At the least let my hand play
In your breast a little way,
Or, if that's good, further down.

1 Classical mythology: Pluto is the god of the underworld and Charon is the
ferryman who carries the shades of the dead across the river Styx.

CXXXVI

It's not just hooks and lures and baited lines
From her fine eyes that draw me to her net,
Whether she's laughing or she's measuring out
To lute's song patterns that her dance designs.

Midnight sees not so many torches shine,
So many sands don't thread Euripus' strait[1]
As beauties blend to make her grace complete,
For which I suffer death a thousand times.

And yet the torment that dries up the spring
Of my life is so pleasant, I can't bring
Myself to rise from weakness that's so sweet.

Instead, may Love grant I still keep when dead
This bitter-sweetness from the wound love made
That while I live's the bedrock of my heart.

1 Euripus is a narrow strait separating the island of Euboea in the Aegean Sea
from Boeotia in central Greece.

CXXXVII

Your eye whose lightning sweeps away my storms,
Your eyebrows, rather, my heart's ruling skies,
Your starry brow, vowed to my Lord, the prize
Where he stows bow and quiver when he disarms;

Your marble throat, where beauty leaves her forms,
Your alabaster chin joy beautifies,
Your ivory breast where all honour lies,
Your heart, my hopes of which turn toils to charms;

You've tempted my desire with such a bait,
To glut my hunger, make my joy complete,
I must see you a hundred times a day,

As if I'm some bird who can't settle down
Without turning towards his fishing ground
And flying back there to seek out his prey.

CXXXVIII

Rise into flight, and with a wing stretched wide,
Forcing through rough winds' insolence and power,
Make, Denisot,[1] your quills sweep up and soar
To Heaven, temple where the gods abide.

Then look there on their godheads, Argus-eyed,
Look on their grace, the knowledge that they share;
To catch my Lady perfectly, take there
The loveliest in your mind's eye for a guide.

After, choose colours from a thousand flowers,
Dilute them in the moisture of my tears
That pour warm from my head continually.

Then, fixing straight before your mind and eyes
The template stolen from those deities,
Paint, Denisot, beauty that murders me.

1   For Denisot see note to IX.

CXXXIX

City of Blois, my Lady's native town,
The home of kings, and where I'd choose to stay,
Where I, still young, saw my will borne away
By a soul-penetrating eye of brown,

It was in you I felt that first flame burn;
In you, I learned the power of cruelty;
In you too that fierce beauty caught my eye:
The memory still makes that flame return.

May Love make his home in your town forever,
And may his lamps, his arrows and his quiver
Hang in you, make his glory's temple there.

And may he always have the right to brood
Over your ramparts with his wings, and, nude,
To wash his curls in the streams of your Loire.

CXL

Happy was that star from which fortune smiled
That marked my Lady with a favouring eye.
Happy the crib, the hand that knew the way
To swaddle her up that day, a new-born child.

Happy was that breast that sweet manna filled
From which she took her first milk hungrily,
How happy the womb that conceived her must be
To bring such beauty, such gifts to the world.

How happy, how honoured, you her parents were
To see her born a favourable star!
Happy these walls, her beauty's native place!

Happy the son whose growth will swell her side,
But happier he by whom she will be made
Woman and mother, where a virgin was!

CXLI

The rising star beneath which I was born
Didn't look out to dominate the skies;
When I was born it was there in your eyes,
Those future tyrants that would keep me down.

My all, my good, my luck, all I have known
Came from your eyes: to forge us stronger ties
Their light in prophesy united us
So as to make us two in essence one.

I am in you, you are in me, just you:
You live in me, and I live in you too,
So perfect is the circle of our love.

Not to live in you would be death to me.
So Pyralids,[1] cast from their fire, would die,
Just as the Dolphin would, cast from his wave.

1 Pyralids were insects believed to live in flames.

CXLII

From the black tresses of your lovely hair
Love wove himself the bowstring for his bow;
He lit his fire from your spark's living glow,
He made his arrow from your eye's brown glare.

His first shot left me feeling death draw near,
His next recalls me from death, pulls me through,
Which treats my ulcer, makes it whole and new,
And by his new shot makes the first shot cure.

So, once before, amid the Trojan dust
The lance from Pelion the Greek hero thrust
Next took the Mysian's agony away.[1]

Just so the bolt her beautiful eye hurls
In the same shot at me both cures and kills.
See what a Fate[2] has spun my destiny!

1 Classical mythology: Achilles (the Greek hero) had a spear, made of wood
   from a tree on Mount Pelion, which wounded Telephos (the Mysian –
   Telephos was a son of Hercules who became King of Mysia) but had the
   power to cure the wound it had made.
2 For Fates, see note to XII.

CXLIII

That smile sweeter than all that bees compose,
Those teeth, rather, two silvered rampart walls,
Those diamonds set in double parallels
In the coral of a mouth red as a rose,

That sweet speech that awakes souls from their doze,
That singing that holds my cares in its thralls,
Those two skies over two stars: all this tells
The world the wonder that is my goddess.

From her young spring's beautiful garden there
Is born a perfume that would scent the air
Of heaven with her sweet breath through all time's changes,

And from there comes the charm of such a voice
As makes the ravished woods leap and rejoice,
Mountains lie low, plains rise to mountain ranges.

CXLIV

In dreams and reveries I'll always come
To the meadow where I saw that angel first,
The source of hope and fear on which I'm nursed,
And whose eyes give my destinies a home.

With what silk thread, plaits spun to coil and roam,
Was her head only that day freshly dressed?
What rose's and what flower's colours graced
Her face that, Iris-like, changed in its bloom?[1]

No way was it a mortal woman I
Saw then, nor could a mortal lady be
Possessed of such a forehead or such eyes.

So, Reason, it was not so strange a pass
If I was caught; a true Angel she was,
Who'd come to capture us down from the skies.

1   Classical mythology: Iris, a messenger of the gods, appeared as the rainbow.

CXLV

My whole mind was dull, sluggish, when I took
From that place that torments me with its sting
The golden orange, like me, ripening
With the same evil we both seem to like.

Apples are presents that Love loves to make.
Warrior Atlanta, you know what they bring,
And Cydippe, whose heart's still sorrowing
At the golden wit that cut her to the quick.[1]

Apples are Love's true sign, so happy he
To whom the apple falls deservedly!
Venus always has apples in her breast.

We've yearned for them since Adam's moral grapples;
The Grace[2] always has them to hand. The rest
Is short: love's just a nice game played with apples.

1 Classical mythology: Atalanta was a virgin huntress who didn't want to
   marry. She would only marry the man who could beat her in a footrace.
   Hippomenes, helped by Aphrodite, used golden apples to distract her and
   so won the race. Cydippe was a girl of noble family tricked by Acontius,
   who wrote a promise to marry him on an apple he rolled her way. She picked
   up the apple, read the legend aloud and was trapped.
2 For Grace see note to XV.

CXLVI

I'm searching, harrowed, for a spring to clear
A horrifying dream out of my mind
That just devoured all night, night without end,
This soul my suffering has steeped in fear.

It made my sweet-inhumane girl appear
To cry out: 'Save me from this danger, friend!
Some unknown bandit's dragging me off bound
Hand and foot through the woods, his prisoner.'

Then leaping up to go where that voice leads,
Cold steel in my fist, I crash through the trees,
But running where the stolen girl might be,

I was attacked by the same bandit there,
Who ran my own sword through the heart of me,
Then dropped me down a waterfall of fire.

Song

My Lady, I'd have never thought,
Seeing how my wasting state persists,
That your heart would reciprocate
With cruel and harsh returns like this,
And that instead of helping me
Your lovely eyes would see me die.

If by some foresight I had glimpsed,
When first I set my eyes on you,
The trouble I have suffered since
For love too faithful and too true,
My heart that till then had lived free
Would not have bowed so readily.

You promised in your lovely eyes,
Eyes that came only to deceive,
To give me a yet greater prize
Than my heart ever hoped to have.
Then, jealous of what I possessed,
They nullified my happiness.

Soon as I saw their beauty then
Love overcame me with desire
To live a loyal citizen
Where their sweet will was Emperor,
And from the look they shed he shot
The first bolt straight into my heart.

Lady, that's how you welcomed me,
Which, to make all my blessings true,
Opened to me with your eyes' key
The paradise that lovers know;
Enslaved in such a blessed abode
I changed – a man turned to a god.

Belonging to myself no more,
But to those eyes that wounded me,
I've left my heart in pledge there for
My faith in their sweet mastery,
Where it knows such sweet servitude
No beauty else could do it good.

And though it suffers day and night
From many forms of love's distress,
The cruellest of its hardships might
Strike it instead as happiness,
And it could never yearn to be
Made suffer by another eye.

A giant rock that has its back
And foot strafed always by the force
Now of the winds, now waves that work
Their anger out against the shores
Won't stand fast as my heart stands firm
Beneath your harshness in its storm.

For it, unchanging, loving still
The lovely eyes that caught it fast,
Resembles diamond most of all,
That, so integrity might last,
Breaks to the hammer when it's hit
Rather than see itself recut.

So gold will never work as bait,
Nor beauty, grace or bearing do,
Ever to plant within my heart
A portrait that is not of you,
And it would sooner die of care
Than suffer any other there.

So there can be no need, to block
Some other Lady's settlement,
To wall it round with massive rock,
Or with a ditch or battlement:
Love's conquest for you there's so full
It can't be retaken at all.

My song, the stars will shine at night
Yet not illuminate the sky,
And sooner winds will cease, forget
To raise their storms across the sea
Before the cruelty of her eyes
Could make my loyalty the less.

CXLVII

A dark veil, glooming the horizon's vault,
Disordered heaven with a sudden flood,
As through the rent air scattered hailstorms poured
On all the fields their random, swift assaults.

Already Vulcan urged his one-eyed dolts
To beat their well-known forges fast and hard,[1]
And Jupiter, concealed within a cloud,
Gathered the lightning of his thunderbolts,

When my girl, walking in her simple dress
Picking the flowers, with the light of her eyes
Swept all the hail and rainstorms far away,

Locked up the winds that had escaped to riot
And made the Cyclopean hammers quiet,
Restored Jupiter's eyes' serenity.

1   Classical mythology: Vulcan/Hephaestos was the god of fire, the great artificer of the gods. He forged the thunderbolts of Jupiter/Zeus in Mount Etna, where the Cyclopes, brutal one-eyed giants, worked under his command.

CXLVIII

Somewhere the twin flames of the girl who'd light
My world have gone to make another day,
Or rather burning noon, that constantly
Glows in the heart and never sees the night.

Ah, why are there not two wings, left and right,
Fledging their feathers either side of me?
Under Love's escort, through the Heavens, high
I'd soar next to her like a swan in flight.

Transfixed by her beautiful rays I would
Empurple all my feathers in my blood
To show what agony I have to take;

And yet I'm certain that my sad decline
Could soften, aided by these sighs of mine,
Not just her heart, but an unyielding rock.

CXLIX

If you don't want to fall from grace with God
Listen to me, and don't shun with a sneer
The humble sigh that is the child of prayer:
Prayer is Jupiter's daughter, so it's said.

Whoever thinks prayer's something to avoid
Never lives all their youth through, free and clear:
They always see their arrogance flung sheer
Down into hell, as punishment for pride.

And so, proud beauty, let that storm pass by,
Temper bravado in these tears I cry,
Show some compassion, cure my wasting sickness.

The winds don't always rage through skies and seas;
Your callous beauty doesn't always need
To probe my wound with such excessive strictness.

CL

Now spring's here why's she not come to my arms,
That girl who keeps my wound forever green,
And strips my thoughts of strength and discipline,
Here on the rug this grassy incline forms?

And why's she not a nymph this green wood claims
As native here? In this cool shadow's screen,
Like a new woodland god, I'd soothe the keen
Rage of my ardour's overpowering flames.

Why, heavens, did your destinies' decree
Not place my birth in errant chivalry,
Who ride with maidens down their lonely roads?

And who with touch, kiss and sweet chattering,
Remote from envy's and from slander's sting,
Live out their lives with them amongst the woods?

CLI

Let all things in this world change utterly:
Let Love have no more appetite for tears,
Let hard oaks have the power to bring forth flowers,
Waters no longer rise when rough winds fly;

Let honey ooze from rock unnaturally,
Let spring have just one colour that it wears,
Summer bring cold and winter heat that sears,
The cloud no longer swell as winds pass by;

Let everything be changed, since that strong knot
That held me fast, and only death should cut,
She's taken the decision to undo.

Why do you so despise the law Love gave?
Why do what no one should have power to do?
Why are you so false as to break your faith?

CLII

Brown-eyed moon, goddess whose black horses take
You round in cycles, high, low, here and there,
And never, coming round, rest anywhere,
But drag your chariot through its endless work,

What you and I desire is not alike:
The loves that score the marks your soul must bear
And passions that goad my soul like a spur
Have different objects their conditions seek.

103

Caressing your Latmian sleeper,[1] you
Would always want a sleep-drenched passage through
To slow your chariot as it flies on by;

But I, whom Love devours all through the night,
From evening on yearn for the dawn, and wait
To see the day that your night hid from me.

---

1   Classical mythology: Selene/Luna, the moon goddess, loved Endymion,
whom Jupiter/Zeus put to sleep on Latmos, a mountain in Caria. She visited
him in his sleep each night.

CLIII

Love's wasting sickness, ever changeable,
Grows green in my soul, never ripening;
Within my eyes there flows a gushing spring,
An Etna makes my heart its furnace fuel.

One with its heat, one with streams running cool
Freezes me, or blasts through me, thundering;
Guerrilla war: now one, now the other thing
Attacks, and neither can impose its rule.

Give, Love, just one control of all this place –
Fine if it's fire, fine if it's chilling ice:
Choose one and put an end to all this bother.

Alas, Love, all I want to do is die.
Two poisons, though, can't kill effectively
So long as each one counteracts the other.

CLIV

Now, since that eye whose influences wield
Power over mine, on mine casts no more light,
Darkness is day to me, my day is night,
So harsh the pain its absence makes me feel.

My bed seems like a hard-fought battlefield;
Everything pains me, nothing brings delight,
And that same thought that's always in pursuit
Squeezes my heart harder than pincers' steel.

By the Loir,[1] amid a hundred thousand flowers,
Choked with anxieties, regrets and tears,
I would have ended all my bitter pain,

Were it not for some god turning my eye
Toward that country where you still delay:
Just the breeze from there makes me live again.

1   For the Loir, see note to XVI.

CLV

As heat on Erymanthos' pinnacle,
On Rhodope,[1] or mountain peaks elsewhere,
Melts, when the springtime comes, cold snows to clear
Streams, turning rocks into a waterfall,

So your eyes (that sun that torments my soul)
That make me wax and snow before their glare,
Striking mine, have distilled them tear by tear
Into a rivulet my sorrows fill.

No flowers or herbs grow next to it, unless
They're marigolds, yew trees and cypresses;
Its banks aren't filled with crystal running free.

Other streams run through meadows, tumbling past,
But this one here flows only through my breast:
It's born out of my pain, and won't run dry.

1 Erymanthos and Rhodope are mountains referenced in classical literature.

CLVI

Let sharp-toothed worries, thousand-headed care
Keep your awakened eyelids without rest,
Black venom keep your lip forever moist,
And writhing vipers cover all your hair;[1]

Let blood in which those fat green lizards share
Infection soil your bosom and your breast,
And with a sideways look, eyes red like rust,
Squint at me to your heart's content and leer;

I'll lift my head to Heaven still, and by
My writings that storm like the tempest, I
Will blast your monsters' powers with my thunder.

As often as you try to teach them ways
To strike at me or pull my stronghold under,
So often you will feel I'm Hercules.[2]

1 Classical mythology: a reference to Medusa; see note to VIII.
2 For Hercules, see note to XIII.

CLVII

From food made out of honey mixed with gall
– The name of it's loving excessively,
Sugar and bitter aconite to me –
I take my sustenance: I'm never full.

That fine brown eye that overpowers my will
On such a diet so starves me away
I can content my hunger just one way:
Only by looking at a vain portrayal.

The more I look the less I'm satisfied,
So I'm a true Narcissus[1] in my need.
Ah, Love! Love's such a very cruel thing.

He'll drive me to my death, I realise;
And yet I can't help my own agonies,
So deep in my veins runs his poison's sting.

1 Classical mythology: for Narcissus, see note to XX. The reference is to his
pining away for an image.

CLVIII

Deluding myself, I trick my own eyes,
Loving a face, a vain projected thing.
What new sensation's this cruel suffering!
Harsh destiny, the malice of the skies!

Must I, my own admirer, come to this,
Loving too much the waters of a spring,
Reason my senses have set tottering
Mistakes its sickness for its highest prize?

And so must my own face's vanity,
Stealing from limb to limb, annihilate me,
Like a wax candle heat's strong rays devour?

107

That's how lovestruck Narcissus[1] wept aloud
When on the damp bank he felt his fine blood
Give birth there to a beautiful new flower.

1   For Narcissus, see note to XX.

CLIX

Wretch, I am happy in my misery,
When the night multiplies the heavens' fires
Or when Aurora[1] strews dawn thick with flowers,
Weaves amaranth through skies like tapestry.

I feed my soul with mourning joyfully,
And anywhere I take my lonely cares,
Forever there before my eyes appears
The girl who raises war and peace in me.

For loving her too much I have to bear
Both pleasure and harsh pain in equal share,
That come marching in step to seize my heart.

In short, my wormwood's so infused with such
A honey, pleasure and pain please as much
As each other, and pain and pleasure meet.

1   For Aurora, goddess of dawn, see note to XCV.

CLX

When Jupiter, his stirring seedtime come,
Yearns to sire his beloved progeny,
And from the heat of his arousal he
Scatters his seed through Juno's humid womb;[1]

When sea, when violent winds give way, make room
For the great warships to sail on their way,
When that bird, in the deep wood's greenery,
Cries out and her Thracian laments resume;[2]

When meadows, and when flowers with myriads
Of colours in a thousand thousand shades
Brighten earth's bosom, painting all the ground,

Alone, in thought, in furthest rocks apart,
I tell my sorrows from a silent heart,
And through the woods I go, hiding my wound.

1 Classical mythology: Juno/Hera is the wife of Jupiter/Zeus.
2 Classical mythology: the nightingale relates to Philomela, who was raped
 by her brother-in-law, Tereus, King of Thrace, and transformed into the
 nightingale.

Madrigal

Cursed be the mirror that reflects your face
And gives your beauty such ferocity,
And so puffs up your heart with cruelty,
Refusing to grant me that longed-for grace!

For three whole years now I've sighed for your eyes,
And yet my tears, my Faith, my Loyalty
Didn't take from your heart (o destiny!)
Sweet pride that caused my martyr's sacrifice.

And in the meantime you don't realise how
This fine month and your years are passing on
Just like a flower that, withering, hangs low,
And how time, once passed, can't be found again.

So while your youth and all its grace remain
And time ripe for love's jousts is left to you,
Don't ever tire of the sweet joys you win,
And don't face death without some love to show.

CLXI

Why don't I hold, Love, this wild creature, as live
In my arms as she's live within my heart?
One moment would cure my long wasting state
And give my pain a haven, make it leave.

The more she runs, more she's a fugitive
Down paths of pride and inflexible spite,
The more I tire, and, as my powers abate,
Plod on behind her, too slow to arrive.

Listen, at least; slow down a little too:
I don't come as a huntsman chasing you,
Nor as an archer, wounding unawares:

But as a friend your love struck violently,
Heart-broken by that shot Love loosed at me,
Forging his arrows from your eyes' fine rays.

CLXII

My heart rose up, rebelled against the sky,
When destiny whose power I can't constrain
Decreed I'd see my Lady once again,
And wear this new rind, physicality.

Heat flowed, marrow to marrow then, through me,
From nerve to nerve and then from vein to vein
And burned my heart; and so I've lived since then
In pleasure now, now in cruel misery.

So that, seeing how beautiful she is,
And how divine, brings back my memories
Of leaving her in paradise before;

For since the day the wound she made returned,
Whether she's near or far, without an end,
She's been the one I, thought and deed, adore.

CLXIII

This is the wood my holy Angel's voice
Fills when the spring comes with her joyful song;
These are the flowers her feet walk among
In solitary, thoughtful reveries;

This is the meadow and the soft bank's rise
Where her hand's touch makes growth spring rich and
strong,
When at each step she hides in her breast new sprung
Flowers, the bright enamel of fresh grass.

I saw her sing here, there I saw her cry,
I saw her smile here, there was ravished by
The things, fatal to me, that she once said;

I saw her sit here, I saw her dance there:
And on the loom of such a vague idea
Love wove my life out of these ends of thread.

CLXIV

My eye was too ambitious, certainly,
Choosing an object of such loveliness,
A virtuous nature worthy a goddess,
Whom even Love's in love with, in his way.

From that day on, this weakness mastered me,
For loving that cruel beauty to excess:
No, not cruel, but sweetly rebellious
To this desire that brings me misery.

No, not misery: happiness, I admit:
It's worth so much to love a girl like that,
The girl I live for: I belong to her.

In pleasing her, I seek out my own sorrow;
I love her so, I've no self-love to borrow,
Though Love drives me for her sake to despair.

CLXV

Sacred Gâtine,[1] who are my anguishes'
Sweet confidant, replying in your wood,
Your voice now high, now low, to match its mood
To those long sighs my heart cannot suppress;

Loir,[2] who restrain your waters' headlong course
From rolling through our Vendôme at the flood
When you hear me speak of that beauty, the food
For which I still starve, growing ever worse:

Now, if I've read the omen skilfully
And my eye wasn't cheated yesterday
By sweet looks my sweet Thalia[3] seemed to fling,

You'll make a poet of me, in death's despite,
And throughout France you'll be called as of right
My laurel,[4] you; you, my Castalian spring.[5]

1 For Gâtine, see note to CXXVI.
2 For the Loir, see note to XVI.
3 Classical mythology: Thalia was the Muse of comedy and idyllic poetry.
4 Classical mythology: for the laurel and its significance, see note to LXXI.
5 Classical mythology: the Castalian spring was a spring at Delphi sacred to
   the Muses and associated with poetic inspiration.

CLXVI

While, Baïf,[1] you strike right in the bull's-eye
Of virtue, where no second stands in line,
And grow drunk gulping waters the divine
Hesiod drank in the Muses' company,[2]

An exile here, where Sabut Hill[3] nearby
Loads up its fertile shoulder with new wine,
I watch, lost in thought, the meandering line
The Loir[4] takes with its tribute to the sea.

Sometimes a cave, sometimes a savage wood,
Sometimes some secret strand, does me some good,
Trying to beguile myself of my vexation,

But though I keep to myself, I lack power
To silence Love or stop him coming here,
So he and I remain in conversation.

1 Jean-Antoine de Baïf (1532–89) was a friend of Ronsard, a poet and a member
   of La Brigade (La Pléiade).
2 Hesiod is the Greek poet, believed to be roughly contemporary with Homer,

the author of *Theogony* and *Works and Days*. The reference is to his having drunk from the Hippocrene spring on Mount Helicon, sacred to poetic inspiration.

3   Sabut is a hill near Ronsard's home near Vendôme.
4   For the Loir see note to XVI.

CLXVII

What good will come to me now, having been
Familiar for so long with her eyes
That could shame the sun with their sparkling lights
Even at the high noon of a summer's reign?

And what pleasure will come now, seeing this fine
Brow, this domed heaven where all beauty lies,
And this white neck that exceeds in its whites
Milk curds heaped on the straw on which they strain?

As that Greek's wandering band of numbskulls, lured
By the sweet taste that lotus flowers afford,
Were glad to eat them and return no more,[1]

So I'm afraid my soul, having acquired
A taste for so rare and so sweet a diet,
Might leave my body and go live elsewhere.

1   Classical mythology: the reference is to the Lotus Eaters episode in the *Odyssey*, where members of Odysseus' crew become addicted to the taste and the narcotic effect of the lotus flowers they eat and no longer want to return home.

CLXVIII

Since I don't have, for making my retreat
Out of this labyrinth where I'm lured astray,
Like Theseus, a thread to lead the way
My wary steps take through the maze of Crete,[1]

Had I at least a breast through which the light
Could pierce, crystal or lucid glass, your eye
Might search inside, read in the heart of me
The kind of faith that makes my love complete.

If you knew the enthralling passion's power
That makes me your perfection's prisoner,
Then death might bring relief to my complaints;

And then, perhaps, as pity seizes you,
You'd heave over my now extinct remains
Some sigh of friendship, though it's too late now.

1 Classical mythology: Theseus, the hero of Athens, killed the Minotaur in the
   labyrinth on Crete, from which he escaped by following the thread given to
   him by Ariadne.

CLXIX

Warm-Welcome,[1] ah, how treacherously your
Sweet talk exploited my youth's innocence,
Leading it to the orchard, out to dance
Love's round, just when I'd passed my twentieth year!

And so Love started off my schooling there,
My master being a thought of little sense
That recklessly led me off down the chains
That linked the maddest dance through its career.

Five years this orchard's inmate, I have gone,
With False-Danger my partner, dancing on,
Holding too sceptical a lady's hand.

I'm not the only one Love's led astray:
The fault's down to my youth, you understand;
I'll be more crafty when my hair is grey.

1 The allegorical names and references to the orchard and the dance here are
taken from the *Roman de la Rose*, a medieval dream vision poem written in
the early thirteenth century by Guillaume de Lorris and continued around
40 years later by Jean de Meun.

CLXX

As I was fencing, freak misfortune pinned
My left arm with a broken sword's sharp thrust,
And so its point, half-blunt, half-jagged, pierced
Me at the elbow, made a bone-deep wound.

My arm began to shed blood all around,
And then the beauty who kills me, infused
With pity, tried with care to staunch it, nursed
And dressed the injury with her own hand.

Alas, if you've some wish to give relief
(I said then) to the wounds that scar my life,
And give it the strength it had at its start,

Don't probe this here, but let your pity keep
On going, to the wound Love scores so deep
With your fine eyes in the core of my heart!

CLXXI

The woodlands' tops aren't always overset
With an eternal winter's weight of snows;
The thunderbolts of justice Godhead throws
Don't always spear down incandescent threat.

The winds, the Aegean Sea aren't always set
To roaring by a cruel storm as it blows;
And yet a constant care's tooth always chews
My wretched life up, leaves it desolate.

The more I will myself to make care die
The more it's reborn for a better try,
Fomenting war in me, war deep within.

Ah, Theban strongman, had your power and faith
In service fought as well that monstrous birth,
Your labours would be numbered to thirteen.[1]

---

1 Classical mythology: the reference is to Hercules and the Twelve Labours.
See note to 'Elegy to Muret'.

CLXXII

I want, so I can fly up to the skies,
To burn all my flawed human skin and bone,
Becoming immortal like Alcmene's son,
Who sat amongst the gods still all ablaze.[1]

My soul already, high in its desires,
A rebel deep within my flesh, moves on,
Now brings wood for its victim's martyrdom,
Self-immolation in rays from your eyes.

O holy firebrand, blaze whose ardours stream
From a divine fire, may your searing power
Burn my familiar corpse with such clean flame

That, free and naked, I leap clear to soar
Beyond the sky, so there I may adore
That other beauty out of which yours came.

1   Classical mythology: Alcmene's son is Hercules. See note to XIII. Hercules,
    after being poisoned by the shirt dipped in the blood of the Hydra which
    was given to him by Deianira, prepared his own funeral pyre and was taken
    directly from there up to the gods, his immortal half unburned by the flames.

CLXXIII

My crazy thought, to fly up ever higher
After the blessing my pride yearns might come,
Is fledged with wings that wax joins to the limb,
Ideal for melting in the first heat's glare.[1]

Agile, he acts the bird, hops in the air,
Vainly pursues his goal of martyrdom,
And you, who can and should have words with him,
Reason, you see it all and you don't care.

Under so beautiful a star's clear light
Give up, Thought, hazarding your wings in flight,
So no one sees your feathers burned away.

To damp down ardour where such burning sears
There wouldn't be enough in my eyes' tears,
Nor the sky's waters, nor waves of the sea.

1   Classical mythology: the reference in the first four lines is to Daedalus and
    Icarus. In order to escape from imprisonment on Crete, Daedalus, the great
    artificer, made wings for himself and his son Icarus out of feathers which
    were attached to the arm with wax. They were successful in flying away
    until Icarus disregarded his father's warning not to fly too close to the sun,
    the wax melted and Icarus fell to his death in the sea.

CLXXIV

Whether the sky is full, whether the ground
Is thick with ice, hail scattered to all parts,
And the horror of the coldest months exerts
Its power to make the plain's hair stand on end;

Whether the wandering riot of the wind
Shatters the rocks, plucks woods up by the roots,
And the sea, redoubling all its baying shouts,
Visits its swollen rage on every strand,

Love burns me, and the icy winter's chill,
That freezes everything, can't freeze at all
This everlasting, raging flame I hold.

So, lovers, see the treatment that I meet:
I die of cold in summer's utmost heat,
And die of heat right at the heart of cold.

CLXXV

I'm not used, Muses, as late evening's haze
Descends, to see you dancing in a ring;
I've never once drunk from the sacred spring,
The offspring the winged horse's hoof-strike raised.[1]

It was the live spark from your lovely rays
Made me a poet: if my voice can sing,
My lyre enchant you with its answering string,
Let your eye, my Parnassus,[2] take the praise.

Heaven certainly owed you to France in debt
When the great Tuscan was allowed to write
Sorgue, Florence and his Laurel in the skies.[3]

119

More than divine in beauty, too late now,
You come to view our age, alas, and how
It's not fit even to speak of your eyes.

1 Classical mythology: the sacred spring is the Hippocrene spring on Mount
   Helicon, which rose when Pegasus' hoof struck the rock. See note to XV. It
   was held to confer poetic inspiration.
2 Classical mythology: Parnassus was the home of the Muses.
3 The great Tuscan is Petrarch, the Sorgue a river in Provence, like Florence,
   his native city, a place with which he is associated, and the Laurel is a refer-
   ence to Laura. See note to LXXII.

CLXXVI

Neither so beautiful a girl's disdain,
Nor joy from melting into languidness,
Nor pride her sweet severity betrays,
Nor her chastity, rebel to Love's reign,

Nor thinking that she's too much on my brain,
Nor the eternal dropping from my eyes,
Nor messengers sent from my heart, my sighs,
Nor her ice feeding an eternal flame,

Nor what rasps me and bites at me – desire,
Nor seeing in my face death written there,
Nor all the wrong turns through a long lament,

Will so fragment my diamond heart that still
Her beauty won't be felt there, and imprint:
'He makes a good end who dies loving well'.

CLXXVII

In the same bed where I rest in the throes
Of thought, swooning near death my Lady lay
Two days ago, when fever wiped away
Her cheeks' carnations and her lips' red rose.

Out of her fevered state moisture arose
That left her poison in the bed for me,
Which, by cruel fate, hurt me a different way,
And down my veins another fever flows.

She felt first cold, then hot: one, then the other.
Neither's relieved in this sickness I suffer,
And when one grows the other grows no less.

Her fever wasn't always on the attack:
Alternate days the heat she felt died back;
What I feel's constant and continuous.

CLXXVIII

O arrows shot to my soul's deepest part,
O mad attempt, O thoughts I've thought again,
O years of my youth that were spent in vain,
O honey, O gall my Lady makes me eat!

O hot, O cold that freeze and fire with heat,
O rash desires, wrecked where no hopes remain,
O sweet wrong turn, tracks in a pointless line,
O mountains, O rocks my pains penetrate!

O earth, sea, chaos, destinies and skies,
O night, O day, O hellish Deities,
O overmastering passion, fierce heart's-fire,

O you Daimons,[1] you holy spirits too,
If ever some love captivated you,
Look, for God's sake, and see what pain I bear!

1   Neo-Platonism: Daimons are intermediate spirits between the human and
the divine, referred to in Plato and in Neo-Platonic thought. They are effec-
tively the same as the Demons referred to in XXXI. See also note to CXCI.

CLXXIX

I must stay quiet even as I blaze,
Because the more I want to quench my flame
The more desire relights fires that have lain
Beneath dead embers where their smouldering dies.

And yet I'm happy, and it gives me peace
To bear yet more than I can bear of pain,
Suffering this sickness of which I complain.
Complain? No, where I see my comfort lies.

Through this sweet sickness I adored the beauty
That binding me around with a meek cruelty
Unloosed me from the bonds of ignorance.

Through this I learned the mysteries of Love,
Through this I learned of hope's omnipotence,
Through this my soul returned to heaven above.

CLXXX

There's a close kinship between Love and Mars:
One fights in open day, one fights by night,
One wounds his rivals, one wounds men who fight,
One break's a household's, one a city's doors.

One winds a fortified town in his snares,
While one beguiles a home in deadly quiet,
One makes the spoils, one victory his pursuit,
One brings dishonour and the other scars.

One beds down on the ground, one often will
Lie at the door, outside, where winds blow chill;
One drinks plain water, one tears, time and again.

Mars walks alone, alone the Loves[1] go their way;
Who wouldn't waste in idleness should be
This one or that: lover, or fighting man.

1 For the Loves, see note to XL, and note to CXIV.

CLXXXI

The time will never come my heart forgets
(Though in the tomb's oblivion I may be)
The memory of her kindly greeting me
That cured my wound and opened it afresh.

This beauty, for whom I brave a hundred deaths,
Meeting mine with her gently smiling eye,
Seemed so sympathetic to my misery
One look repaid for all my wretchedness.

And so, if just a long-hoped-for good day,
Full of sweet kindness, after long delay,
Bathes my hopes in a hundred nectar streams,

Then to what paradise would I be brought,
If arm to arm, bound in a true love's knot,
I held her, even only in my dreams?

CLXXXII

Alone, I suffer, and no one can know
Without being me the pain I have to bear:
Too sharp for me, Love, like a thief, makes clear
Away with my heart: I can't have it now.

I never should have abdicated so
Much to the enemy who wields such power,
But from the first I should have kept him near
So reason might tell duty what to do.

Well, it's done now! He's set off down the track;
The times are passed when I could drag him back;
He's wilful, with the reins at his command.

I know he's carrying my life away.
I see my blunder, and yet I'm carefree,
'Death comes so beautifully at your hand!'

CLXXXIII

Deep in a valley all enamelled round
With a thousand flowers, I glimpsed her far away
Whose beauty penetrates the heart of me,
And then pain creased my brow into a frown.

Seeing the dense woods, the low-lying ground,
I armed my heart with fresh temerity
To sing to her the wrongs she sends my way,
The torments in me her sweet eyes bring down.

A hundred ways already my weak tongue
Was trying to frame its opening harangue,
To lighten my pains of a little weight:

But then a Centaur,[1] coveting my life,
Snatched her onto his back and galloped off,
Left me alone, left my cries incomplete.

1 Classical mythology: centaurs, half man and half horse, are associated with
   the snatching away of human women, as in the famous battle with the
   Lapiths depicted on the Parthenon friezes.

CLXXXIV

House widowed of my Lady's lovely eyes
That feed me pain whether they're far or near,
I think you're like some meadow out of flower,
Some body orphaned by its soul's release.

Is heaven's crowning glory not that blaze
That gives both light and heat for all to share?
Isn't your greatest ornament the power
Of her fine eye, whose impulse leaves me dazed?

Let all your sideboards groan with heaps of gold,
All your re-tapestried walls once more hold
Embroidery and gold thread intertwined.

All that, House, gives me no cause to rejoice
Unless I see that Lady, hear her voice
That I still hear, and see within my mind.

CLXXXV

Seeing that today, to give my pain some ease,
My Lady gave me some locks of her hair,
I now forgive you, heart, for laying bare
My inmost stronghold to my enemies.

It's not hair but a strong network of ties
Love binds me with and Heaven makes me wear;
Freely I yield myself up, captive there
In such fine tresses, bonds where my death lies.

Hair of such blonde profusion doesn't deck
Delos-worshipped Apollo's[1] milk-white neck,
Nor does the flame-hair of the Egyptian queen,[2]

When the stars wear its firelights for a crown,
For all night's darkness, rival in its sheen
These lovely knots in which my arms are bound.

1 Classical mythology: Delos was sacred to Apollo.
2 Classical mythology: Berenice was a queen of Egypt who dedicated a lock
   of her hair at the shrine of Aphrodite to her husband's safe return. When the
   lock of hair disappeared Conon of Samos suggested it had been taken into
   the skies to form a new constellation, which still bears Berenice's name.

CLXXXVI

I was sure, at this changing of the skies,
This new year would turn my fate, make it break,
And that its path, that wound round like a snake,
Would soothe my careworn labour's miseries.

But since snow and rain are its chosen guise,
Giving a damp day its long face to soak,
That told me in the course this year would take
I'd pour my life away, out through my eyes.

126

O you who are the quintessence of me,
Whose humours sway mine with their mastery,
Calm all my troubles with those eyes of yours,

Or make my eyes distil into a spring,
To drown all of my love and suffering
In the river to be born out of my tears.

CLXXXVII

Spiteful Aglauros,[1] with your soul that's rife
With envy, with your scandal-dripping tongue,
For having dared to publish to the throng
The secret that I held dear as my life,

May fierce Tisiphone[2] wreathe your neck, grieve
You with remorse, with care, with sorrowing,
With flame, whip, snake and arrow, following,
Punish your madness and give no relief.

To avenge me, may this toxic verse I write
Trace all the horrors of the furious spite
With which Archilochus[3] made iambs kill.

May my fierce rage weave you a noose from that
Murderous thread Lycambes,[4] jealous still,
To save himself, pulled tight around his throat.

1 Classical mythology: Aglauros was the daughter of Cecrops, turned into
   stone by Mercury/Hermes for frustrating out of spite his abduction of her
   sister.
2 Classical mythology: Tisiphone is one of the Furies, the avenging spirits who
   pursued malefactors in retribution for their crimes.
3 Archilochus (c. 680–c. 645 BC) was a Greek iambic poet notorious for the
   power of his invective.
4 When Lycambes refused his daughter to Archilochus, the story goes that the
   resulting iambics drove him to suicide.

CLXXXVIII

As Virgil sang, there's not one place on earth
Where faith is sure, and what made me believe
Was your young heart, old in power to deceive,
Proving too fragile in love, breaking faith.

You wouldn't know, woman of little worth,
How to subject hearts to the power you have,
Wind's plaything, sea too subject to each wave,
Beauty too lovely for a soul too blithe.

Love, listen: if there was a time you'd hoist
Aloft in flight on the wind of my voice,
Never see my heart and hers reuniting.

And may the Heavens fix her tongue and fire
The sharpest of their triple-pointed lightning
Down on it, as fair payment for its hire.

CLXXXIX

Her head is gold, her brow's a painted scene
Where I can see the profit from my loss;
Beautiful is her hand, premature cause
In me of change in colour, hair and skin.

Beautiful is her mouth, her eyes' twin sun,
Snow and flame come to beautify her face
For which Jupiter would assume the dress
Of a swan's plumage or bull's hide again.[1]

Sweet is her smile, enough to harden, lock
Even Medusa[2] in some ghastly rock,
Avenging at once a hundred thousand cruelties.

But just as the sun rises to outshine
The lesser lights, so does this faith of mine
Exceed all the most perfect of her beauties.

1 Classical mythology: Jupiter/Zeus transformed himself into a swan to court
   Leda, and into a bull for Europa.
2 For Medusa see note to VIII.

CXC

What sways the Maenads to insanities
Can't always cloud every bewildered brain;
And they can't always stamp, to the trumpets' strain,
The hills of Troy in choric lunacies.

The god of wine-enraptured Thyades
Can't always spur their hearts till they're insane,
And there are times their minds, where manias reign,
Cease raging and show no signs of disease.[1]

Even the Corybantes sometimes rest,
And Curetes, lithe under each armed crest,
Don't always feel the goddess goad and sting.[2]

But what this girl moves in me, love's mad fever,
Won't leave me one hour free of suffering,
And from her eyes it wounds my heart, forever.

1 Classical mythology: the Maenads and Thyades were priestesses of Bacchus
   famed for their god-crazed dancing rampages round the countryside.
2 Classical mythology: Corybantes and Curetes were priests of Cybele who
   danced in armour in caves under the possession of their goddess.

129

CXCI

Although the fields, the rivers, every place,
The mountains, woods I've left behind back there,
Distance me far from my sweet Warrior,
Star of fate, source of my best destinies,

Some Demon,[1] with permission from the skies,
Who ruled over my primal passion's fire,
Flies always on his well-worn path to steer
Her lovely image home into my eyes.

All through the nights, impatient in my haste,
I feel again, once more my arms embrace
Her hundred shapes warped from delusion's mirror.

And when he sees me sleeping happily,
Shattering my joy, he flies off, waking me
Alone in my bed, filled with shame and terror.

1 Neo-Platonism: for Demon see note to XXXI and note to CLXXVIII. The
reference here is to the depiction in some Platonic writings of Demons as
tutelary spirits to specific individuals, or even as abstract powers within
individuals that drive them on.

CXCII

Hot weather, and sleep like a running tide
Suffused my soul that dreams had charmed away,
When a vague simulacrum came in play,
Sweetly bewitched me as I slept that night.

Stretching beneath me, lovely, ivory white,
She snaked her writhing tongue all over me,
Her delicate lips kissed me constantly,
Mouth on mouth, body pressing body tight.

What coral, lilies, roses – petals, flowers –
Did I seem then, as handfuls fell in showers,
To feel amid our mutual fondling there?

My God, my God, what a sweet-tasting breath,
What scented exhalations filled her mouth,
What rubies and what diamonds there were!

CXCIII

These twin waves of milk here compacted thick
Move over their white valley, back and forth,
As on its shore the sea, salt on its breath,
Slowly goes out, and then comes slowly back.

An empty space extends between them, like
A pass between two mountains, a level path
Whitened by all the snow that fell to earth
When in the wintertime the wind fell slack.

Two rubies redden there, set proud and high,
The gleam from which completes this ivory,
Curving and smoothly rounded on all sides.

And there all honour, there all grace abounds,
And beauty, if this world has some around,
Flies home to that beautiful paradise.

CXCIV

What sickness tarnishes this lovely brow?
By what dark veil is this flame's light decreased?
What pallor draws blood from this lovely breast,
That stands up to Aurora,[1] blow for blow?

God of Healing, if there still lives in you
The old fire that Thessalian shrub once raised,[2]
Come help this young complexion, do your best,
Touch its pale lily till carnations show.

And you, bearded Aesclepius, faithful guardian
Over the Ragusins, your Epidaurians,[3]
Quench my life's torch that burns out of control!

It lives, I live; I'm nothing if it dies;[4]
As her soul is united with my soul,
My destinies follow her destinies.

1 Classical mythology: for Aurora see note to XCV.
2 Classical mythology: the god of healing is Apollo and the Thessalian shrub
   a reference to Daphne, pursued by Apollo and transformed to a laurel.
3 Classical mythology: Aesculepius is a patron god of medicine, and
   Epidauros, sacred to him, was the home of the Ragusins.
4 Classical mythology: the hunter Meleager was prophesied to live only until
   a particular burning brand was consumed by the flames: his mother,
   Althaea, put it out. Later, when he had killed his brothers, she put it back
   into the flames again to kill him.

CXCV

From Spain's shores, where the day's confined in night,
As far as India, there grows no flower
To rival in its beauty, grace and power
The lustrous colouring of Marguerite.

No orient jewel that's so rich (so bright
Her radiance, fuelled by happiness, can flare)
Encrusted with its pearl the conch shell where
Venus, still young and small, first saw the light.

Nor purple sprung from blood Adonis shed,[1]
Nor the mournful *ai! ai!* of Ajax dead,[2]
Nor the great haul of jewels that India fetches,

Nor all the treasures brought from foreign shores,
Could match their value in exchange for hers
In the least aspect of her twofold riches.

1   Classical mythology: when Adonis (see note to XCIV) was killed by a boar, his blood, sprinkled with nectar by Venus/Aphrodite, gave rise to the anemone.
2   Classical mythology: Ajax, the 'Great' (not the Ajax referred to in CV) committed suicide and from his blood sprang a red flower (a hyacinth) which showed on its petals the letters 'ai', a lament.

CXCVI

Into my dead breast, to the depths of me,
I feel as if a hand is reaching in,
Ransacking me, to pull back out again
My captive heart it rules and drags away.

You evil custom, wicked in your way,
Unwieldy law, the cause of so much pain,
You've killed me, you go so against my grain,
Mere human law, too harsh, too strong a stay;[1]

133

Must I, the loner thousandfold cares bite,
Brood on this empty bed so many nights?
What hatred I bear, ah, what envy rips

Through me for Vulcan[2] here, who, pitiless
And graceless, blocks the light my soul's half sheds,
Placing the sun of my life in eclipse.

1 Ronsard is referring here to marriage.
2 Classical mythology: Vulcan/Hephaestos was the husband of Venus/
Aphrodite, a pattern for the deceived and jealous husband.

CXCVII

Give me my heart, girl, give me back my heart,
That your breast keeps there in captivity;
Give me, give me back my sweet liberty
That (fool) I gave your lovely eyes to guard;

Give me my life back, or delay death's start,
Who while I love your beauty chases me
Out of some principle of cruelty,
And take a closer look at how I hurt.

If death's how you reward my wasting sickness,
The age to come, deploring your harsh strictness,
Will say above you, 'May a hard rest grieve

The bones of this loved girl who proved so fierce,
And who once cruelly murdered with her eyes
One who held her more dear than his own life.'

CXCVIII

When the day's eye arrives in Gemini
A gentler daylight soothes the universe,
The green fields ripple with corn's tufted ears,
Banks paint their colours with fresh artistry.

But when it slips obliquely, slowly by,
Rolling along the Zodiac's sideways course
To Sagittarius, change for the worse
Takes daylight, flowers and beauty clean away.[1]

So when my goddess's eye casts its light
Within my heart, there grows within that heart
A crop of lovely thoughts to buoy me up.

But then, as soon as that ray takes its flight,
My thoughts turn barren and bear no more fruit,
And my hope's cut down without growing ripe.

1 The references are to the sun's passage through the zodiac as a calendar of
   the year. The sun enters Gemini around 20th May and Sagittarius around
   20th November.

CXCIX

Follow me, page boy: where the grass grows higher
Reap the bright colours the green season strews,
And scatter then in fistfuls through the house
These flowers that April while she's young can bear.

Hang from some nearby hook my singing lyre:
I want to charm, if I can, the poisonous
Spell a fine eye that witched my reason used,
For which her ruling glance supplied the power.

Bring me ink and bring paper too: there on
A hundred sheets, proofs of the cares I've born,
I want to trace what I endure, this pain;

A hundred sheets – tougher than diamond stuff –
So that one day a future race of men
Might judge the wrongs I suffer as I love.

CC

Lines read at random out of Homer's verse,
By destiny, coincidence or chance,
Sing in my favour without dissonance –
Tell how the pains I suffer will find cures.[1]

These Greybeards, who come to predict the course
Of the future from our looks – face, carriage, hands –
Foretell as they pass the relief that ends
Sufferings that pain so bitter to me stirs.[2]

Even at night, sleep that brings you to me
Sweetly into my bed, by augury
Promises me I'll see your spite turned mild,

And you alone, the oracle of love,
Will someday come into my arms to prove
So many prophecies at last fulfilled.

1 Picking lines at random out of classic books was a form of divination used
   in the Ancient World.
2 Ronsard's 1553 annotator Marc-Antoine Muret (1526–85), a Latinist with
   close links to La Brigade (La Pléiade), suggests that the Greybeards are
   gypsy fortune-tellers.

Madrigal

A stupid Vulcan drove my Venus mad:[1]
Weeping, and not one to conceal her ire,
She armed one of her eyes with sparks of fire,
Poured over her cheek tears the other shed.

Meanwhile, Love, who was small enough to hide
In beauty's breast like some bird in her care,
Passing the damp eye, bathed his wing in there,
Stood by the hot one till his feathers dried.

You see such an ambivalence of face
When spring sun all at once can laugh and cry,
Combining either mood ambiguously,
When there's a cloud that's passing half across.

What sorrow mingled with what sweet reward
Was it to see how she moved, and the tears
She shed, full of regrets that Heaven heard?

1   For Vulcan see note to CXCVI.

CCI

Oh Love, what sorrow, what dissembled tears,
What sighs my Lady fashioned as she went,
And what sobs, as her anguish came to paint
A colour of death on those charms of hers!

Hands folded on her chest, she looked to pierce
Slowly to heaven with a fixed intent,
She spoke in tears so sadly her complaint
Shattered the rocks that were her listeners.

The Heavens, halted by her sorrowing cries,
Changing complexions, colours, tendencies,
Fell sick with it all out of sympathy.

137

Flame-headed stars, their brows all furrowed, shook
Their lights out then, so pitiful a look
Swam in the crystal of her moistened eye.

CCII

My Lady's twin stars of fire burned away
With the bright ray cast from their sacred flame
The tearful build-up of dark, drizzling rain
Which was obscuring the light of their day.

A lovely silvering, running moltenly
Over her cheek, her ivory breast, came
Down to her chaste heart's beautiful domain
Where the Little Archer honed his armoury.

The whole of her face was full of warm snow,
Her hair gold, ebony her double brow,
Her eyes were glittering like a fatal star,

Roses and lilies, where her mouth contained
The grief that formed her note of just complaint,
Fire in her sighs, a crystal in each tear.

CCIII

He who made this world, fashioned faithfully
Along the lines his ideal patterns trace,
Setting its crown, his temple vault, in place
Ordained that I'm your slave by destiny.

Just as the soul that's born in sanctity
To see its God, when it looks on His face,
Can have no happier gift, no ampler grace
Granted to it than just to look and see:

That's how my customary pain withdraws
When my eye drinks long draughts of light from yours,
That masterpiece beyond comparison.

That's why, wherever that eye may be found,
Always, despite myself, I turn around
That way, as heliotropes follow the sun.

CCIV

Sweet Sleep, that brings to everything its peace,
Brings no peace to the care that snatched my sense:
I die in you, live only in you, hence
See nothing but you that has power to please.

Your eyes threw into my heart coals that blaze
So hot, a flame's pursued me ever since,
And since the day I saw you in the dance,
I'm dying for you, yet I'm quite at ease.

From hurt to hurt, one worry to another,
I've a sad soul, a body chilled all over,
Never to warm the coldness of your ice.

At least read what's here on my brow, and see
How many deaths your sweet looks make me die:
'Care hidden can be recognised on sight.'

CCV

If I'm not blamed now as I used to be
For physical and mental idleness,
Give credit to the bolt from your bright eyes
That smoothed rough edges of my soul away.

Their graceful flame casting a single ray,
Lifting my bold flight in the air, to rise
And see the Whole, raised me up to the skies –
That Whole whose part down here sets fire to me.

Through lesser beauty that gave wings to thought
My thought flew up to beauty's inmost heart,
Spurred by obsession far beyond all help.

There I adore true beauty in perfection,
There all my idleness was turned to action,
And there I knew my Lady and myself.

CCVI

Ferocious North Wind, Scythia's bitter breeze,
Chaser of clouds and shaker down of rock,
Enrager of sea, making one part knock
At Hell's gate, hurling one up to the skies,

If beautiful Orithyia's[1] memory stays
With you, agent, archer of Winter, make
My Loir[2] take all the threats it poses back
Until my Lady's left its waterways.

If you do, may your brow never be wet
And may your hideously blustering throat
Bellow on through deep caverns endlessly;

140

May branches on the oldest oaks we have,
Just like the earth, the sea, the skies above,
Tremble with dread wherever you pass by.

1 Classical mythology: Orithyia was abducted by Boreas, the North Wind.
2 For the Loir, see note to XVI.

CCVII

Sister of Paris, Asia's royal girl,
Within whom Phoebus, though misgivingly,
Planted the spur to know all, recklessly,
From which no good came when it seized your soul,[1]

You'll change to me out of capricious will,
Since now you're pleased, late though it is, to be
Looking to change your Loire for my Loir,[2] stay
There where your choice of home happens to fall.

Heaven is on my side to guide you here,
To show to you from closer up the care
That paints its true life colours on my face.

So come, Nymph, come, and all the rocks and woods
That flame with pity to my voice's moods,
Weeping the pain I feel, will warm your ice.

1 Classical mythology: the references in the first four lines are to Cassandra's
   status as a princess of Troy and the dubious gift of prophecy given to her by
   Apollo. See Introduction.
2 For the Loir, see note to XVI.

CCVIII

The curling gold I value all the more
As my pains grow out of its loveliness,
Slipping one day out of her headband's ties,
Fanned out across the breast that I adore.

My heart I now call back in vain (despair!)
Flew into it just like a young bird does
That, flying deep inside a bush, then goes
Flitting at will from branch to branch in there.

Ten fingers, ten ivory branches, then
Gathering her lovely hair's strands back again,
Caught my heart in their snare that drives me mad;

I saw it but I had no power to cry,
Dread so tongue-tied me, simultaneously
Freezing my heart and the unspoken word.

CCIX

He must hide lead or wood behind his face
Who doesn't feel the fear and wonder thrill
When face to face he sees my matchless girl,
Or when he hears her voice's harmonies;

Or when, thought-led through the loveliest month's days,
Alone she walks the gardens, Love her sole
Confidant, as her rosy hand picks all
The sweetest budding flowers to make bouquets;

Or when the summer, as its heats abate
At evening by the door sees her transmute
Silk into gold, such is her thimble's skill,

Then with her rose-outblushing fingers play
Her lute, and with one turn of her eyes, steal
Hearts from a thousand men as they pass by.

CCX

With all its flowers and buds just freshly blown
The beautiful spring makes pain spring in me,
In each nerve, every vein and artery,
Fanning a fire that burns me to the bone.

Sailors don't count so many waves being thrown
Ashore when Boreas[1] breathes most bitterly,
Nor's Africa so full of sands, as my
Heart numbers torments that it keeps locked down.

Desire would master me, I've so much grief,
A hundred times a day to cut this life,
Mining the stronghold of my weakened state,

Were it not for my trembling with the fear
That after death I'd have no wound to bear
From that death-blow that's so sweet to my heart.

1   Classical mythology: Boreas is the North Wind.

CCXI

Never so blonde, so lovely as this fleece,
That kills my sorrow and makes pleasure gain
On me, was that gold bulls that spells turned tame
Gave up to Jason on the fields of Mars.[1]

And those who live in Tyre, their chosen place,
Never wove such a fine silk on the frame,[2]
Nor woodland moss sheathing the bark could claim
Such softness as this in the spring's prime days.

143

Hair worthy to crown the goddesses' heads,
Since you leave your comrades to join me instead,
My heart feels hope creep in and start to stir.

Take courage, Love, the town's already captured
When it splits in two, mutinously fractured,
One faction yielding to the conqueror.

1 Classical mythology: in the legend of the Golden Fleece, Jason was ordered
   by Aeetes, King of Colchis, to yoke two fire-breathing bulls as a task he must
   accomplish to win the fleece. Aeetes' daughter, Medea, who loved Jason,
   was an enchantress who prepared a spell to tame the bulls.
2 Tyre was legendary for the production of purple dye and fabrics.

CCXII

It's not some vapour trapped beneath the ground
That gives rise to such storm winds in the air,
Nor with its floods does the impetuous Loir,[1]
Spoiling our crops, engulf the fields around.

These aren't the months Prince Aeolus[2] sets unbound
The captive pride of winds that bluster and roar,
Nor Ocean[3] turns his giant key to pour
Tempestuous waves from springs where they're contained.

My sighs alone have brought this wind to life,
The Loir grew swollen with my tears of grief
At seeing so wild a beauty up and go,

And I'm amazed my sighs and tears have been
Continuing so long, yet I've not seen
How these are wind and those a river now.

1 For the Loir, see note to XVI.
2 Classical mythology: Aeolus was the ruler of the winds, and kept them
   imprisoned, except during the times when they were allowed to be let loose.
3 For Ocean, see note to X.

CCXIII

I've more joy than the gods here in my heart
When, Lady, you give me your burning kiss:
Your kiss – so sweet and yet so larcenous –
Steals me bewildered up to Heaven's gate.

So kiss me then, my heart, because I rate
Your simple kiss higher than some goddess
Holding me naked in a close caress,
Her shapely arm clasping our love-play tight.

Yet always it's your custom that your pride
Adds to your kiss some bitterness beside,
Cold, foul; if not, such luck for me would be

Unbearable; my soul, as it reached out
To a thousand beauties, would fly through my mouth
And I'd die on your breast from too much joy.

CCXIV

I feel, portrayed in memory, every part
Of you: your long hair, your mouth and your eyes,
Your sweet look and your conversation's grace,
Your sweet ways and the sweetness you impart.

Unique Janet,[1] France's hero of art,
Could pencil nothing that better portrays
These than the deft strokes that the Archer traced
Painted their vivid memory in my heart.

So in my heart, carved in a diamond,
I have her portrait my love sets beyond
Even my heart itself. Vivid portrayal!

Janet's power to make images will die:
Yours in my heart will take my death away,
So life goes on even beyond my burial.

1 Janet is the nickname of François Clouet (c. 1510–72), a leading portrait painter at the French court with particular skills in portrait drawing.

CCXV

Dexterous Helen, needle in her hand,
Retraced the battles that her husbands fought
On linen:[1] on that point, you make good sport
Working the wrongs with which my life is crammed.

But Lady, for all that your wool, your strand
Of black thread, sketch death that awaits me out,
Why don't you work the other way about,
Shade in some green a hope my pain might end?

My eye sees nothing on your tapestry
Save black, save orange, sad embroidery
To evidence long sufferings I bear.[2]

Cruel fate! Not only does that eye of hers
Undo me so, but everything she does
Holds no promise for me except despair.

1 Classical mythology: Helen of Troy is shown in the *Iliad* (Book 3) as stitching a tapestry which depicts the battles going on around her with one husband, Menelaus, on the Greek side, and another, Paris, on the Trojan side.
2 References to colours relate to their symbolic meanings. Orange was associated with the melancholy lover.

CCXVI

Love, how I love to kiss my girl's fine eyes
And with my mouth to twist round and about
The fine gold of her hair that tangles out
And down her brow that's starlit like the skies!

To me the best of her best points is this,
Her beautiful eye, that touches my heart,
Whose lovely clustered jewels could impart
To the wildest Scythian's[1] heart charm and grace.

Her lovely gold hair, her eyebrows as well,
Could shame Aurora,[2] they're so beautiful,
When in the morning she lights up the day.

From its home in her eye a power's evinced
That goes out swearing by Love's arrows she
Will cure me: I remain, though, unconvinced.

1   Scythians were considered to be ferocious barbarians.
2   For Aurora see note to XCV.

CCXVII

The bow that brings the bravest troops to terms,[1]
Which pays no heed to breastplate nor to shield,
With such a sweet shot made my courage yield
That on the field there I gave up my arms.

My constancy has never raised alarms
While I've lived as Love's slave; nor could it; held
Captive, I'd only ever tears to wield,
My sole support should I pursue my aims.

And all the same, my rage seethes at the thought
Of being defeated, right at the first shot,
Without resisting longer in the war;

But my defeat deserves high dignity,
Seeing that the king – no, god – who's captured me
Fights Heaven above, Hell down below, Earth here.

1   The bow is Love's, and the reference in the last line is to Love, who has
defeated Jupiter in Heaven, Pluto in the underworld and men on earth.

CCXVIII

That eye that gives joy to this world of mine,
That turns whoever comes close into rock,
Now with a smile, now with a savage look,
Feeds my heart, whether peace or discord reign.

Through you, sweet eye, I'm silent in my pain;
But then, as soon as I feel my grief strike,
Beautiful, sacred, angel's mouth, you make
Me, by that sweetness you have, live again.

So, mouth, why do you come supporting me
With your fine speeches when I want to die?
Why do you want me living as before?

Good soil for trouble, I revive and linger,
A true Prometheus,[1] so that care once more
Can come, feed on my heart a little longer.

1   For Prometheus, see note to XII.

CCXIX

Since that day I first breathed a captive's sighs
The serpent year's turned seven times about:
Yet now, such stars reigned when I took the bait,
I'm martyred worse than those first, fevered days.

Back when I'd read, then with a student's eyes,
Florence's poet[1] voice his tragic fate,
I couldn't, in my disbelieving state,
Contain the laughter of my mockeries.

I was so green I never thought at all
Some man might have felt things I couldn't feel,
And I judged others by what I had been.

But the little Archer who got mad with me,
To punish me, hid such a bolt away
Inside my heart, I've known no joy since then.

1 Florence's poet is Petrarch.

CCXX

When I see you talk, quite carried away,
Wholly beguiled by some thought of your own,
Your head lowered a little, looking down,
Withdrawing from the vulgar herd and me,

I often want, to break your reverie,
To call out to you, but my tortured groan,
Blocked up there, overawed, a heap of stone
In my mouth, leaves me standing wordlessly.

My dazzled eye cannot withstand your gaze;
My soul is moved to trembling by its rays;
Neither my tongue nor voice gains any traction.

Only my sighs, just this sad face I have
Speak for me then, and such a painful passion
Gives ample testimony of my love.

CCXXI

Artery to artery and vein to vein,
From nerve to nerve her greeting shot through me;
That's how my Lady just the other day
Left me all sad at heart there, all alone.

It was so sweet for me I can't remain
Silent – it shed such stings as she went by,
Wounded me with its bolt so grievously,
It left an ulcer where my heart had been.

Her eyes, her voice, her gracious movements all
Fell into time and harmony so well,
My soul filled with such hunger for such joys,

That whether it, craving a taste so sweet,
Tearing all its terrestrial bonds apart,
Might leave me, was in doubt a thousand ways.

CCXXII

Sweet girl, what are you saying, trying to do?
What are you dreaming? Don't you think of me?
Do you just not care for my anxiety,
While my care for you pierces me right through?

My heart boils over with my love for you,
You're there before my eyes incessantly,
I hear you, catch your voice when you're away,
There's no love but this my thoughts echo to.

I have your beauties, your graces, your eyes
Graven in me – every spot, every place
Where I saw you dance, speak and laugh out loud.

I keep you mine, and if I'm not my own,
It's you in whom my heart breathes, you alone,
My eye, my blood, my bane and all my good.

CCXXIII

Forget now, potent god of herbs that heal,[1]
The cruel trick my girl played on you not far
From Hellespont,[2] and lend a prompt hand here
To cure her colour fevers now turn pale.

Make her beautiful, dying body whole!
It would be, Phoebus, a great shame to bear
Should weakness, for lack of your help, outwear
The eye that kept you pining such a while.

If, to oblige me, you pity her plight,
I'll sing how Delos,[3] wandering isle, struck root
At your command into the sea beneath,

How Python[4] was your maiden conquest, how
Then Daphne[5] gave the tresses on your brow
This honour – their first ornamental wreath.

1 The poem is addressed to Apollo, or Phoebus. See Introduction.
2 Classical mythology: Hellespont is the strait near which Troy stood. The
   Trojan Cassandra offered herself to Apollo in return for the gift of prophecy
   but did not keep her part of the bargain.
3 Classical mythology: Delos was a floating island that took root at the birth
   of Apollo there.
4 Classical mythology: Apollo killed Python at Delphi.
5 Classical mythology: Daphne was turned to laurel so she could elude
   Apollo's pursuit.

CCXXIV

Although your arrow, Love, flies all too true,
And you yourself are filled with fraud and spite,
In living to serve you, Love, I've had quite
Good fortune in the camp that follows you.

This beauty that sets me to pining – no –
Who doesn't want me just to pine without
Reward, as I kissed her, told me I ought
To cut a love knot from her gold hair now.

I was so honoured, even with her own
Scissors I cut it. See the lengths love's gone,
See, Lovers, what great wealth fell to my share.

So in my verses may I never fail
To glorify those scissors, that hair as well –
My agent here and my true love knot there.

CCXXV

If I break free from stocks that fetter me,
Stocks where Love shoots his bolts to nail me through,
Escape clean from this snare that binds me too,
And see myself untangled, my neck free,

At a field's heart, with people far away,
One that the Loir's[1] forked arms clasp in its flow,
I vow a temple built of turf to you,
Fortunate, holy and sweet Liberty.

There I'd hang, high up on the chancel's wall,
A sacred image, as a sign to all
Lovers, so they don't follow where I went.

And, to keep me from once more falling back,
I'd kill a Hecatomb[2] for the gods' sake:
'He who reforms in life makes a good end.'

1   For the Loir, see note to XVI.
2   A hecatomb is a sacrifice of a hundred bulls.

CCXXVI

Seeing the pain gently wear me away,
That's step by step my faithful follower,
I quite foresee how I'm still not yet there
At my verse end – I love excessively.

Lady, what fires my soul to sing this way,
And makes me less tired of my labour here,
Is seeing how you hold my singing dear,
And how your uppermost thoughts are of me.

I'm happy, Love, my happiness runs over
To live beloved, and to live as the lover
Of beauty in so beautiful a Lady,

Who reads my verses with true judgement, whose
Eyes give me all the reasons I can use
To breathe my sighs for her, and breathe them gladly.

CCXXVII

Playfulness, Grace and the two Loves,[1] the twins,
Follow my Lady, and where she goes round,
Beneath her feet enamel all the ground,
And out of winters they create new springs.

It's for her that the birds chirp jargonings,
Aeolus[2] locks his winds deep underground,
Sweet Zephyr lets out a sweet, plaintive sound,
And dumbstruck brooks silence their murmurings.

The Elements see themselves new in her.
Nature laughs, seeing such loveliness appear.
I tremble that one of those Deities,

Fired by her lovely face with passion's rage,
In plundering the treasures of our age,
Might snatch her up and take her to the skies.

1 For Loves see note to XL, and note to CXIV.
2 For Aeolus see note to CCXII.

Kiss

When from between your opened lips,
As from between two beds of flowers,
That rose-tinged exhalation slips,
My lips, my kiss's couriers,
Blush red with pleasure at your breath,
And all my longing overflows
In raptures as I kiss your mouth,
Because that kiss's moistures soothe,
Drop by drop, falling to the heart,
The brasier where love's hot coals seethe,
The flames of which your eyes ignite.

Elegy to Cassandra

O my Cassandra, eye, heart, life of me –
It's only right you should feel jealousy
Towards this great king, whose will won't endure
Your name being my song's burden any more.[1]
It's he who wants me to exchange my lute
For a trumpet fit to blare great fanfares out,
Not just for him, but all his ancestry,
Who sit above, ranked with the gods on high.
I'll do the job, since he commissions it,

Because the power of such a king's so great
It's ineluctable – by such a distance,
An army couldn't offer true resistance.
   But what help's having read so much Tibullus,
Propertius, Ovid, erudite Catullus,[2]
Seen so much Petrarch, studied it so hard,
If I'm by royal appointment disempowered
From following their path, and if my lyre
Must hang on a hook and dare speak no more?
   And so I fed on hope, then, pointlessly,
That one day I might prove to Tuscany[3]
That our France is as blessed as she in sighs
Expressed in sorrow for love's agonies;
To show the way she could be put to rout,
I'd already begun by drafting out
Many an elegy in the ancient style
And many a fine ode and pastoral.
   Because, to tell the truth, I'm still not smitten
With any of the poets who have written
In our French language, and their songs of love
Rate close to zero, or not much above.
   It's not that I'd be so vainglorious
As to dare boast I'd beat the laboured verse
So many lovers, weeping through France, tried;
But at the least my hopes seemed justified
That, if my verses didn't come in first,
They wouldn't be dishonoured as the worst.
(Erato,[4] who reveals love's poetry,
Set me to work with an approving eye.)
   One sings his poems coarsely, too inflated,
One drags on in a low style, enervated,
One paints a lady who freely inclines,
One cares more for his verse than what it means,
And none of them, for all their fancy dress,
Could ever learn to do what Petrarch does.
   Why do you cry, Cassandra, my sweet soul?
Love has no wish yet to cut down the wool
I hung up on the loom here for your sake

Without completely finishing the work.
    My king hasn't been suckled by uncouth
Wild creatures, and the vigour of his youth,
If I'm not wrong, has sometimes felt the stings
Of Love's fierce bolt that overmasters kings.
    If he's felt that, then all my guilt's assuaged,
Nor will his greatness be provoked to rage
If, back from battles and their hideous strain,
I take my lute down off its hook again;
And, strumming, in place of alarms and fears,
I sing of Love, your beauties and my tears,
'Because the bow that's drawn too roughly either
Loses its spring or shatters altogether'.
    Just so Achilles,[5] leaving warriors killed
And strewn so thick back on the battlefield,
Picked up his golden lute with that same hand
That still all those inhuman murders stained,
And, sitting with Patroclus face to face,
Sang of his love for his girl Briseis,
Then suddenly picked up his arms again –
Back to war, even braver than he'd been.
    That's how, after my Master's ancestor
Withdraws his sword-arm from the bitter war,
And disarms in his tent somewhere remote,
Then, right on time, your Ronsard, with his lute,
Will sing of you, as it can never be
That any other beauty takes his eye,
Whether he's still alive or Charon's[6] brought
Him dead, light cargo, out beyond the port.

1   The king referred to is Henri II. In writing the *Franciade* (see note to LXXI, and Introduction) Ronsard would be writing about Henri's supposed mythological ancestors.
2   Tibullus, Propertius, Ovid and Catullus are Latin poets associated particularly with love poetry.
3   References to Tuscany allude to the Petrarchan tradition on which *Les Amours de Cassandre* is based.
4   Classical mythology: Erato was the Muse of lyric poetry, especially love poetry.

Classical mythology: the reference to Achilles singing to his friend Patroclus about the loss of the slave girl Briseis adopts the characters from the *Iliad* but does not refer to any specific incident there, but rather to a mention of the event in Ovid's *Tristia*, Book IV, I.

6 For Charon see note to LXX.

Elegy to Muret[1]

No, Muret, no, it wasn't just today
The archer boy who fires our agony
Caused this confusion that makes fools of men;
No, Muret, no, we're not the first, my friend,
In whom his bow hid, with a small, sharp shot,
So great a wound here, underneath the heart:
All animals – those in the countryside,
Those in the woods, those the high mountains breed –
All feel his power, and his fire's bitter-sweetness
Burns the sea monsters underneath the waters.
   Is nothing left unburned by that boy's fires?
The sky-lifting giant-killer Hercules[2]
Took his full force; Thebes' strongman, understand –
Who strangled the wild boar with his bare hands,
Killed Nessus, and who swung his club to beat
The Centaurs, the cloud's children, to dead meat;[3]
Astonished all of Lerna with his bow,
Took prisoner the dog from Hell below,
Took, on the river bank of Thermodon,
The belt the virgin he'd subdued had on;
Killed the sea monster, and several times over
Mocked all the swerves of Achelous' river;
Who made Medusa, Phorcys' daughter, die,[4]
Who smashed the lion's jaws so violently,
Picked up and crushed Antaeus in his arms,[5]
And set two pillars up, to stake his claims.[6]
   In short, this hero who fixed the world's faults,
This fearless heart, war's very thunderbolt,
Felt that god's power, and love's fire, ravaging,

Bowed him down more than his taskmaster king.
Not lovestruck like we're lovestruck, the world's wonder,
You with your Janne[7] and me with my Cassandra,
But pricked by Love with such a gadfly goad,
His whole fanatic heart boiled, overflowed
With sulphur that burned, cauterised his veins.
They were so choked with smoke where love's fire ranged,
And so choked were his bones, muscles and nerves,
That Hercules, who purged the universe,
Had nothing left but love's insanity,
Poured through him from the eyes of Iole.[8]
   Always he loved Iole's lovely eyes,
Whether the chariot that lights the skies
Rose from the waters or, descending, spun
Its wheels along the salt sea's level plain,
Resting all mankind from work's weariness,
But not the wretchedness of Hercules.
   Not only did his Lady's eyes fix all
Their power in the profound depths of his soul,
But all – her speech, grace, sweetness – every part
Forever stuck, adhering in his heart.
   His soul contained no thought but that of her:
When she was gone he always saw her there.
And when you see her, Hercules, as fate
Decrees, your voice sticks in your stammering throat,
Frozen with fear seeing that beloved face.
Now fever that your love ignites would rise,
Devouring your soul, now ice floes assemble,
And love's cold shoulder comes to make you tremble.
   Down at your feet, your murderous club is laid
Idle, dishonoured, by the shaggy hide
That bristled stiffly up along your back
When monsters faced your punishing attack.
   But now your frown no longer threatens them:
What wasted powers, what unnatural shame,
And vile disgrace, as Hercules is foiled
And humbled, after conquering the world,
Not by Eurystheus' or cruel Juno's will,

But by the hand of just a simple girl.
     For God's sake, see what power Love has to wield,
When once it's made the tower of reason yield,
Leaving no portion of ourselves behind
Save what's all turned to fever in the mind.
     And that's not all: he didn't just forget
For love's sake how to lay his weapons out,
Or how to heft his dangerous club again,
Or how to fight adversity and win;
But letting cool with sloth and vanity
The heart with which he'd conquered tyranny,
The terror of the world – humiliation –
He dressed himself up in a woman's fashion,
And, from a hero turned a blushing girl,
He plied the needle, turned the spinning wheel,
And in the evening, like a serving maid,
Gave piece-work back to his sweet prison guard,
Who held him shackled in his bonds much tighter
Than any prisoner in an iron fetter.
     Great Juno, your revenge is now complete,
Seeing his life turned idle and effete,
To see transformed like this into a spinster
Great Hercules, the slayer of every monster,
Without your untamed rage being supplemented
With tasks his brother Eurystheus invented.
     What more do you want? Iole requires
His sex change: she's the one he doubts and fears.
He's more scared of her hands than some slavish waster
Of a valet fears beatings from his master.
     Meanwhile, as all he does is think of ways
To dress, anoint himself, accessorise,
To preen his lovely topiary of beard,
To dress his beautifully barbered head,
The monsters go unpunished, at their leisure,
Free to subject the whole world to their pleasure,
Caring no more if Hercules existed.
And that's because of how the poison that twisted
And bored into his heart too far, deep down,

Had killed him in a body that lived on.
　　So we, Muret, who feel that passion craze
Our courage, drive us on to reckless ways,
Let's, if it's possible, escape this bond
Designed for us that Venus' boy has wound,
And drive the flesh that dominates us back,
To set it under sacred reason's yoke –
Reason, that ought to lead us to true good,
And reign as mistress of our sensual side.
　　But if Love, with his arrow's tameless power,
Has put our wound already past all cure,
So far, this sickness better promptings reach
So seldom scorns all reason has to teach,
Let's know we're beaten, give desire its place
And model our own lives on Hercules;
And in this time, while wrinkles don't yet show
Their furrows carved through the fields of our brow,
And snows that come to our old age have yet
To wrap their permafrost around our head,
Let not one day of ours flow into nothing
Without pursuing Love: it's not unfitting
But honourable to one in our low station
To follow the great lords in emulation.

1　For Muret see note to CC.
2　Classical mythology: this poem contains an ironically flavoured account of
　a number of legends relating to Hercules, including some of the Twelve
　Labours. These were labours set by Eurystheus (his brother) at the
　prompting of Hera/Juno, traditionally numbered as follows: (1) the killing
　of the Nemean lion; (2) the killing of the Lernaean hydra; (3) the capture of
　the golden hind; (4) the capture of the Erymanthian boar; (5) the cleaning of
　the Augean stables; (6) the killing of the Stymphalian birds; (7) the capture
　of the Cretan bull; (8) the theft of the mares of Diomedes; (9) the taking of
　the belt of Hippolyta, Queen of the Amazons; (10) the taking of the cattle of
　Geryon; (11) the theft of the apples of the Hesperides; and (12) the capture
　of Cerberus.
3　Classical mythology: a reference to Hercules' killing of the centaur, Nessus,
　and to the killing of other centaurs which occurred in the course of the
　capture of the Erymanthian boar.
4　Classical mythology: the reference to Medusa (see note to VIII) is a little

obscure: she was killed by Perseus, but in another legend was powerless to harm Hercules in the underworld.

5 Classical mythology: this is a reference to Hercules' wrestling match with the giant Antaeus, who derived his strength from contact with his mother Gaia (the earth), and was defeated when Hercules lifted him off the earth and crushed him in his arms.

6 Classical mythology: the Pillars of Hercules are the straits of Gibraltar, in one story formed by Hercules smashing through the mountain that had been Atlas. They represented the western limits of the classical world, and, metaphorically, the limits of knowledge.

7 Janne seems to be the woman loved by Muret.

8 Classical mythology: this is a reference to Hercules' humiliating subjection to Iole, who dressed him in women's clothes and herself took his club as revenge for the death of her father, Eurytus, in the version of the tale used in Ovid's *Heroides*, 9.

Song

> Laurel sticking in her throat,
>   Crying out,
> My Cassandra, in Lycophron,[1]
> Could be heard to prophesy
>   To all Troy
> What would cause their towers to burn.
>
> But those poor, obstinate men,
>   Destined then
> Not to heed their Sibyl's warning,
> Saw, though after many years,
>   How Greek fires,
> Raging, set their city burning.
>
> Death in every heart, they stood,
>   Hands' dull thud
> Bruised each bare chest as they grieved,
> Crying, tearing grey hair out,
>   Each long shout
> Weeping that they'd disbelieved.

Yet they couldn't make their cry
    Mollify
Greeks so heaped with spoils of war
They left nothing to remain
    Save the name
Of what had been Troy before.

I'm the same to disbelieve,
    Now when you've
Told what pain my fates bequeath,
How I'll have nothing to show,
    Quid pro quo,
Loving you, save a harsh death,

Restless wildfire, raging on,
    Every bone,
Every nerve, heart, burned away.
For your love, then, all my share
    Is more fire
Than burned disbelieving Troy.

1   Lycophron is a Hellenistic Greek poet from around the third century BC, the supposed author of a fragment called 'Alexandra', which consists of a prophecy spoken by Cassandra. Laurel in her throat relates to the chewing of laurel leaves by the Sibyls to put themselves into their prophetic trance.

CCXXVIII

My Des Autels,[1] who have since childhood days
Drunk from the waters that flow from the peak
Where the nine sisters[2] in a cavern make
Their home, alone, afar, a sacred place,

If at some time the power of love has graced
Your brows with myrtle[3] planted for love's sake,
As you adored those lovely eyes that take
Through what you write our France's highest praise,

162

Take pity on my wretched languishing,
And soften the heart, with the songs you sing,
Of one who keeps my freedom in constraint.

If at some time I'm there in Burgundy,
I'll melt with my verse, if the power's in me,
The cruelty of your beautiful Saint.[4]

1 Guillaume Des Autels ((1529–81) was a poet linked to La Brigade (La Pléiade).
2 Classical mythology: the nine sisters are the Muses.
3 For myrtle, see note to LXXI.
4 Saint was the name given to the Lady Des Autels referred to in his love poetry.

Song

From that day I became a lover,
No food, however fine the flavour,
No wine, however delicate,
Gives any pleasure to my heart;
Because since that time nothing I
Could eat or drink agreed with me.
A sadness locked up in my soul's
All that I've fed on, nothing else.

All pleasures that appealed to me
When I was love and fancy free
Are now just things that I abhor:
So fencing's no fun any more,
And tennis, hunting, dancing pall;
Instead, like some wild animal,
I shelter, hiding while I rave,
Lost in some unfrequented cave.

Love was so poisonous to me
It charmed my reason clean away,
And took the strength that made me bold,
The mask I used to face the world,
Making me one who shuffles on,
Sad, thoughtful, my head hanging down,
Like I'm a frightened man and dare
Not trust anything any more.

Ixion's[1] storied torments can
Come nowhere near my passion's pain,
And I'd choose rather to endure
Tantalus'[2] fatal sentence for
A year than be in love a day,
To languish so unhappily
As I have, since Cassandra took
My heart and wouldn't give it back.

1   For Ixion see note to XI.
2   For Tantalus see note to XLIV.

Elegy to Janet,[1] Painter to the King

Paint for me here, Janet, paint for me, please,
Onto this canvas, my girl's loveliness
In just the way I'll point it out to you.
I won't beg, as some tiresome bore might do,
For you to make art lie, to flatter her:
It's quite enough if you can paint her there
Just as she is, not looking to disguise
Her natural beauties with mere flatteries:
That only works well with the kind of girl
Who paints herself, and isn't beautiful.
   First paint her hair that falls in waves and hangs
Coiled, curled and twisted, spirals down in rings,
The colour of which is like cedar wood;
Or spread it out and let the scent that's freed

164

Breathe through the picture, if you have the art,
The very scent that her own hair imparts,
Because her hair smells like the flowers that blow
In spring, when Zephyrs fan them, fluttering through.
　　Don't let her lovely brow be lined or cracked
With any furrow, any deep-scored track,
But paint it like the waters of the sea
When they're unruffled by wind's mutiny,
And lying in their bed they're laid asleep,
Soothing the waves dead calm has shuttered up.
　　There, in the midst of her hair's strand-line, let
A lovely ruby hang, whose flashing light
Spreads through the picture, as at night you see
The shining brilliance of the lunar ray
Light up the snows on a sunk valley floor
Where human feet have yet to tramp their spoor.
　　Next paint her lovely eyebrow's arch, as black
As ebony, let it stretch and bend back,
A crescent moon that shows through cloud its shining,
Horn-profiled arc just as its month's beginning.
Or if you've ever seen the bow of Love,
Take your sketch from the semi-circular curve
It traces, making half a perfect ring,
For Love's bow and her brow are the same thing.
　　But, Janet, I'm so wretched, I don't know
What painterly techniques you'll use to show
(Even if you had Apelles' artifice[2])
The natural grace of her lovely eyes,
That put to shame all of the heavens' stars.
Let one be gentle and the other fierce,
One take Mars and one Venus for its guide;
Let all hope shine out from the kinder side,
And from the cruel side darken all despair;
Give one a pitiful and weeping air,
Like Ariadne's[3] when she, left behind,
On Dia's shores, driven out of her mind,
Consumed herself in tears next to the sea,
Calling her Theseus unavailingly;

And make the other bright, just as you would
Believe worthy Penelope[4] once had,
When she saw, back at last, her husband there,
Having spent twenty years away from her.
  Next paint her ear, round, exquisitely made,
Small, even, half white and half pink in shade,
Which gives, from underneath her veil, the look
A lily has, set in a crystal block,
Or looks for all the world just like a rose
In all its freshness sealed in under glass.
  But you'll have wasted all the time you've spent
Making your painting rich in ornament
If you've not painted something that portrays
Just right the line of her beautiful nose.
So paint it neither short nor aquiline,
But neat, well-formed, so one envy inclined
To find fault had no choice but to take it back,
So perfectly your line will make it track
Its way down her face, as a small incline
Descends from where it overhangs a plain.
  Next, paint me to the life her lovely cheek,
Whose colour's a rose floating on a lake
Of milk, or that shade so near white you'd think
A lily had just kissed a blushing pink.
  In the middle paint a dimple on each side,
No dimple, but the place Love goes to hide,
Out of which that boy's little hands let fly
A hundred shots, and not one pointlessly,
That doesn't reach the heart straight through the eyes.
  But Janet, to paint her mouth right, alas,
Scarcely could Homer in his verse dictate
The shade of red you'd need to equal it,
Because to paint her mouth the way it's worth
Depicting, you should paint a Grace's[5] mouth.
So paint it for me there so it might seem
To speak, sometimes to smile, sometimes perfume
The air with some ambrosian exhalation.
Above all, though, make it seem that persuasion

Is filling it with all its gentle power.
And set, a millionfold around it there,
Smiles and allurements, jokes and courtesies,
And make two rows of seed-pearls beyond price,
Evenly set there where teeth might be seen,
Be perfectly formed and arranged within.
    And paint around them then a pair of lips
That of their own accord rise to be kissed,
Inciting it, their colour equalling
Either the rose, or coral's flaming pink,
Rose flaring on the thorn when springtime's here,
Or coral blushing on the ocean floor.
    Then paint her dimpled chin, and at the end,
Show how it forms an apple's curve, a round
Convexity just like that you might glimpse
Forming the end of a new-growing quince.
    Yet whiter than curds of milk on the straw
Paint then her neck, but paint it quite long, draw
It out, slim, soft; and her feminine throat
Should be, like her neck, a bit lengthened out.
    And then give her true measure, set in place
Elbows and arms just like those Juno has,
Minerva's beautiful fingers, and then
Hands like those of the Goddess of the Dawn.
    I don't know, Janet, where I've got to now,
I'm baffled and struck dumb: I don't know how
To point out like before what's left to see
Of beauties that are not revealed to me.
I never was so favoured, I confess,
As to see, naked, her beautiful breasts.
If we can judge by guesswork's evidence,
Persuasive reasons leave me quite convinced
That beauty that lies hidden ought to be
At the same level as that you can see.
So paint that beauty: give it perfect lines,
So it's as perfect as the other kind.
    So draw her torso in voluptuous style,
Fine, white, well-formed, broad, twin-breasted and full,

167

Through which a thousand vessels branch and bud,
Pulsating with their fill of live red blood.
    And then, when your life drawing skills define
The muscles and the nerves beneath the skin,
Form two fresh apples' contours on that base,
As when you see two new green fruits that grace
An orange tree, and till this very hour
The blush has never reached their tip before.
    Paint at the tip of either marble dome
The place the sacred Graces make their home,
Let Love incessantly go fluttering
Around them, brood them, fan them with his wing,
Thinking he's flying with his trickster brother
From branch to branch through orchards on Cythera.[6]
    Then, like a convex mirror, lower down,
Dimpled, plump, softly curving out and round,
Like Venus' belly, paint her belly there;
Then paint her navel, that small centre, where
The inside shows a richer colour than
A lovely pink-flower, favourite of the sun.
    What more's left? Paint that other part for me –
So beautiful, whose name I dare not say –
My urgent longing for which cuts me through;
But don't cover it up, I beg of you,
Unless it's with some sheer, thin, silken veil,
So, through transparency, it's visible.
    Let her thighs be well-turned and rounded out,
Full in their flesh and even all about,
Like an artfully sculpted statue holding
Its firm support beneath some royal building.
    Then draw her knees like two hills raised aloft,
Slim, fleshy, round, perfectly formed and soft,
Beneath which give her a full, well-toned calf,
Of the same kind the Spartan virgins have,
Who by Eurotas lock their arms around,
Wrestle and throw each other to the ground,
Or hunt, their baying packs unleashed, in chase
Of some old stag through woods near Amykles.[7]

Then, for her portrait's final touch, reveal
There Thetis'[8] narrow foot and slender heel.
  Her portrait's nearly done: I see her: yes!
Just one more brushstroke, one more – there she is!
Lift off your hands – my God! She's there, I see!
She isn't far short of speaking to me.

1 For Janet see note to CCXIV.
2 Apelles was a painter of legendary skill from ancient Greece who flourished
   during the fourth century BC.
3 Classical mythology: Ariadne was the daughter of Minos, King of Crete. She
   loved the Athenian hero Theseus and helped him in the killing of the
   Minotaur – see CLXVIII. However on their return to Athens their ship was
   blown off course to Naxos, for which Dia is an ancient name. Theseus and
   Ariadne were drugged and fell asleep there and Theseus was visited in a
   dream by Dionysus who claimed Ariadne as his wife. Athena then appeared
   to Theseus when he awoke and instructed him to abandon Ariadne there.
   Ariadne awoke to find him gone.
4 Classical mythology: Penelope is the faithful wife of Odysseus, to whom he
   returned after twenty years away at the Trojan War and in the wanderings
   of the *Odyssey*.
5 For the Graces, see note to XV.
6 Classical mythology: Cythera is a Greek island sacred to Venus/Aphrodite.
7 Eurotas is a river and Amykles a town in Sparta.
8 Classical mythology: Thetis is a sea nymph, mother of Achilles.

CCXIX

I went rolling these tears out of my eyes,
Now filled with doubt, now full of hopeful plans,
While Henry, far beyond the bounds of France,
Avenged the honour of his ancestors;

While, arms victorious, he cut down to size
Spain's courage in the Rhine-washed hinterlands,
Already tracing with his pointed lance
A royal road to lift him up to the skies.[1]

You, sacred band,[2] my bedrock and my crown,
Whose beautiful flight raised my mind up high,
If there was one time you let me gulp down

The waters Hesiod drank in his day,[3]
May this sigh be forever graven on
The holiest altar raised to Memory.

1   The references are to Henri II's campaigns against the Spanish in Germany
    around 1552.
2   Classical mythology: the sacred band is the Muses.
3   For Hesiod see note to CLXVI. The waters he is supposed to have drunk are
    from the Hippocrene spring – see note to CLXXV.